THE CURSE OF DEMAGOGUES

THE CURSE OF DEMAGOGUES

---

*Lessons Learned from the
Presidency of Donald J. Trump*

Collected Essays

Edited and with an Introduction by Eli Merritt

spotlight
press

ISBN 979-8-9872952-0-5

Contents

Contributors

Jill Abramson is a journalist who spent seventeen years in senior editorial positions at *The New York Times*, where she was the first woman to serve as Washington Bureau Chief, Managing Editor, and Executive Editor. She is also a former political columnist for *Guardian US*.

Michael Austin is the author of six books, most recently *We Must Not Be Enemies: Restoring America's Civic Tradition*. He is a provost, vice president for Academic Affairs, and professor of English at Newman University.

Frank O. Bowman, III, is Curators' Distinguished Professor at the University of Missouri School of Law and the author of *High Crimes & Misdemeanors: A History of Impeachment for the Age of Trump*.

Curtis A. Bradley is Allen M. Singer Professor of Law at the University of Chicago Law School. He is the author or editor of a number of books, including, most recently, *International Law in the US Legal System*. From 2018-22, he was a co-Editor-in-Chief of the *American Journal of International Law*.

Michael A. Cohen is a columnist for MSNBC and writes the political newsletter *Truth and Consequences*. He has been a columnist for the *Boston Globe* on national politics and foreign affairs. He is also the author of *American Maelstrom: The 1968 Election and the Politics of Division*.

Barbara Comstock is an American attorney and politician who served as the U.S. representative for Virginia's 10th congressional district from 2015 to 2019. A member of the Republican Party, she was a member of the Virginia House of Delegates from 2010 to 2014.

Joseph J. Ellis is an American historian whose book *American Sphinx: The Character of Thomas Jefferson* won a National Book Award. His book *Founding Brothers: The Revolutionary Generation* won the 2001 Pulitzer Prize for History. His most recent book is *The Cause: The American Revolution and its Discontents*.

Jeff Flake is an American politician and diplomat who is the current U.S Ambassador to Turkey. He served in the House of Representatives and the Senate, representing Arizona. He is the author of *Conscience of a Conservative: A Rejection of Destructive Politics and a Return to Principle*.

Megan Garber is a staff writer at *The Atlantic*, where she covers culture. She is the recipient of a Mirror Award for her writing about the media, and she previously worked as a reporter for the Nieman Journalism Lab and as a critic for the *Columbia Journalism Review*.

Bryan Garsten is professor of political science and the humanities and chair of the Humanities Program at Yale University. He is the author of *Saving Persuasion: A Defense of Rhetoric and Judgment*.

Jennifer Mercieca is a historian of American political rhetoric, as Associate Professor of Communication and Director of the Aggie Agora, at Texas A&M University. She is also the author of, most recently, *Demagogue for President: The Rhetorical Genius of Donald Trump*.

Eli Merritt a psychiatrist and political historian at Vanderbilt University. His book *Disunion Among Ourselves: The Perilous Politics of the American Revolution* is scheduled for publication in the spring of 2023. He is the editor of *How to Save Democracy: Advice and Inspiration from 96 World Leaders*, also scheduled for publication in 2023. He writes a Substack newsletter entitled *American Commonwealth*.

Yaël Ossowski is deputy director of the Consumer Choice Center. He was previously Watchdog.org's Florida Bureau Chief, chief Spanish translator, and national investigative reporter from 2012-2015. He is also a co-host of Consumer Choice Radio.

Darryl Paulson is Emeritus Professor of Government at USF St. Petersburg. He specializes in the politics of Florida and the South and has served as an expert witness in numerous cases involving voting rights and election integrity, including challenges to Florida's Fair Districts Amendment.

Eric Posner is an American lawyer and legal scholar who has served as a counsel for the Department of Justice Antitrust Division since 2022. He is a professor at the University of Chicago Law School, and the author, most recently, of *The Demagogue's Playbook: The Battle for American Democracy from the Founders to Trump*.

Fredric C. Rich, formerly an international lawyer, writes about contemporary political and moral issues. He is the author of *Getting to Green, Saving Nature: A Bipartisan Solution* and *Christian Nation*, a novel.

James Risen, a former *New York Times* reporter, is *The Intercept's* Senior National Security Correspondent. Risen also serves as director of First LookMedia's Press Freedom Defense Fund, which is dedicated to supporting news organizations, journalists, and whistleblowers in legal fights.

Michael Signer is an attorney who has written three books, including *Demagogue: The Fight to Save Democracy from Its Worst Enemies* and, most recently, *Cry Havoc: Charlottesville and American Democracy under Siege*. He served as mayor of Charlottesville during the years 2016-2018.

Andrew Sullivan is a political commentator, a former editor of *The New Republic*, and the author or editor of six books. He is the founding editor of *The Daily Dish* and has been a regular writer for *The New York Times Magazine*, *The Atlantic*, and *Time*, among other publications.

Andrew Trees is an adjunct history professor at Carthage College and author of numerous books, including *The Founding Fathers & the Politics of Character* and *Club Rules*.

Jesse Wegman is a member of *The New York Times'* editorial board and the author of the book *Let the People Pick the President: The Case for Abolishing the Electoral College*. He was previously a senior editor at *The Daily Beast* and *Newsweek*, a legal news editor at Reuters, and the managing editor of *The New York Observer*.

Richard Ashby Wilson is Associate Dean and Professor of Law and Anthropology at the University of Connecticut School of Law and author of *Incitement on Trial: Prosecuting International Speech Crimes*.

THE CURSE OF DEMAGOGUES

"Democracy begets tyranny through demagogues."

> — Michael Signer, *Demagogue: The Fight to Save Democracy from Its Worst Enemies*

"This book is an attempt at understanding what at first and even second glance appeared simply outrageous."

> — Hannah Arendt, *The Origins of Totalitarianism*

Introduction

by Eli Merritt

Since Donald J. Trump announced his candidacy for president in June 2015, commentators and analysts have been fumbling for the right word to describe him. Some refer to Trump as an "authoritarian" in one breath and, in the next, an "autocrat." Others jump from "strongman" and "dictator" to "fascist" and "tyrant" as they search for the most accurate term. Ultimately, the problem with these labels is not that they are wrong about the underlying potentialities of the 45th president. The tragedy of these descriptors is that they lack the precision we need in an enlightened democracy to identify and rectify the system flaws that led to Trump's rise to power in the first place. As the Renaissance humanist and scholar Desiderius Erasmus put it more than half a millennium ago, "Prevention is better than cure."

The pointed focus of these essays on Trump as a "demagogue" is not meant to invalidate the myriad other labels experts apply to him. The intention is to hammer home a fundamental truth about democracy, one that requires readers to appreciate the significance of word choice when it comes to prevention. It is that stable, functional democracies are degraded by demagogues in a two-step process well-known to political philosophers since the birth of this free form of government in the 5th century B.C.

The first step in democratic breakdown is the election of a demagogue to a high office like the U.S. presidency. Then, once in office, the demagogue devolves into authoritarianism, dismantling the democracy itself to retain and aggrandize power. Perhaps Alexander Hamilton described it best in Federalist No. 1 when he cautioned Americans in 1787 to study history carefully in order to discover the chief danger to representative government. That danger, Hamilton wrote, is demagogues because this species of political actors achieves elected power by manipulating and deceiving the people, "commencing demagogues, and ending tyrants."

Trump commenced a demagogue, and, as the 2022 hearings of the U.S. House Select Committee to Investigate the January 6th Attack on the United States Capitol vividly attest, he ended an authoritarian, orchestrating a multifaceted campaign to overturn a free and fair election. What the United States and the world have witnessed in Trump's political behavior is precisely the two-step process of democratic deterioration Hamilton and so many other experts on democracy warn about. The fact that Trump commenced a demagogue teaches us something urgent about how to protect democracy from self-sabotage. We must thwart demagogues because they, unlike run-of-the-mill authoritarians, possess both the rhetorical genius to get elected and the underlying ruthless personality type that wrecks democracies. It is fair to say, as a rule of thumb, that all demagogues are authoritarians, but not all authoritarians are demagogues. What non-demagogue authoritarians lack is the charismatic ability to get elected.

Trump was the first full-blown demagogue to become president of the United States. He did it by fostering division and distrust in the American people. He did it by exploiting xenophobia, chauvinism, and racism. He did it through character assassination, conspiracy theory, and outright lies. A demagogue, as Eric A. Posner, a contributor to this volume, explains in his book *The Demagogue's Playbook*, is a political actor "who obtains the support of the people through dishonesty, emotional manipulation, and the exploitation of social divisions; who targets the political elites, blaming them for everything that has gone wrong; and who tries to destroy institutions—legal, political, religious, social—and other sources of power that stand in their way."

To understand the system flaws that enabled Trump to win the presidency, we must first acknowledge a fundamental principle that governs the operation of democracies. Demagogues are as ancient as democracy itself, and, historically, watchful gatekeepers have worked to keep them from the bully pulpit and the public trust. Gatekeepers of democracies that survive know that they must keep demagogues out of positions of power. They have eagle eyes for spotting this troublesome subset of political actors, and, by all means permissible, public and private, they labor to sideline them.

Since the founding of the United States, American gatekeepers of the presidency have included constitution writers, elected and appointed officials, political parties, national committees, nominating conventions, the courts, activist elder statesmen, ministers, and journalists, among others. Today the all-important category of journalism encompasses everything from newspapers, magazines, television, and radio to podcasts, Facebook, and Twitter. All these media outlets, as beneficiaries of the freedoms and rights bestowed upon them by the Constitution and Bill of Rights, are necessary gatekeepers of American democracy. Whether they accept the responsibility or not, they are charged with the public duty of counteracting the ascent of demagogues.

Some observers might protest that this critical mission of democracy—blocking a specific subset of political actors, demagogues, from achieving election to high office—is anti-democratic. But this is hardly the case because a cornerstone of all successful democracies is vigorous checks and balances to prevent abuse of power and assault on institutions. In this regard, gatekeeping systems that thwart demagogues are more than essential to democracy; they are the very salvation of our liberties and freedoms. A fundamental truth about democracy is that, unguarded, this form of government slides into tyranny, due largely to its susceptibility to demagogues. This is the abiding paradox of democracy. It is democracy's "inconvenient truth"— its heavy burden and greatest responsibility.

Like it or not, the need to insulate the government from demagogues is the realpolitik of democracy. "We the People" are sovereign. "We the People" do possess the power. But if public-spirited gatekeepers do not corral the candidates, separating out demagogues from the rest, a formerly ethical and tranquil democratic system of government can spiral into institutional breakdown—and violence. That is precisely what happened during the four years of the Trump presidency.

In this spirit of understanding, *The Curse of Demagogues*

has three primary aims. First, it constitutes a short history of Trump's years in the White House (and his first two campaigns for president) as told from the perspective of scholars, journalists, and legal experts who specifically warned the public about his dangers as a demagogue in real time. In reading these pieces now, it is clear that American political thinkers possess the knowledge and wisdom necessary to shield our democracy from usurpation and corruption by executive office demagogues. The question is whether the political and media leadership of the nation today, Republican and Democrat, will heed the warnings and take action to safeguard the system. Demagogues can be found at every level of democratic government, but the United States must train its attention with laser focus at the top, the presidency, where the greatest power is held and therefore the greatest damage inflicted.

Second, this collection is a detailed primer on demagogues and the multifarious ways they poison the vital organs of constitutional democracy. In the pages that follow, writers from diverse academic backgrounds depict how demagogues manipulate both party and populace into outright contempt and violation of the Constitution and rule of law—and into violence. For one thing, demagogues pronounce the opposition to be a mortal threat to the fabric of the nation. They turn the people against one another and undercut rational democratic deliberation, invoking fear and paranoia against "the other." A running theme in many of these pieces, expressed well before the January 6 attack on the Capitol, is the violent nature of demagogues. They use words that inflame the baser passions of their followers, driving them to violent acts.

Michael Signer, a writer of numerous essays in this volume, distinguishes populists from demagogues in his book *Demagogue: The Fight to Save Democracy from Its Worst Enemies*. Signer says that populists play by the rules and adhere to the rule of law whereas demagogues, who are "intrinsically violent," do not. "Hard" demagogues, according to Signer, outright violate rules, norms, and laws. For this reason, they are the battering rams that break down democracies, eventually transforming them into violent authoritarian regimes. Expressed succinctly in a five-word phrase reminiscent of Hamilton's

Federalist No. 1, Signer crystalizes the downward spiral of democracy into tyranny in this way: "Democracy begets tyranny through demagogues."

Third, *The Curse of Demagogues* is an urgent call to study, debate, research, learn, and, critically, to restore gatekeepers to their essential role as defenders of democracy against demagogues. Today, it seems, Americans have lost their way in a polarized and demagogic system of government and media. The best way out of the pit, perhaps the only way out, is to prioritize the study of democracy above all other societal pursuits. We must research and debate democracy and demagoguery with vigor and urgency—with the goal of preserving our liberties and freedoms while simultaneously adapting our political system to the hypersonic digital communications of the 21st century. We must relearn the vital lesson of the ages that democracies must actively struggle against demagogues—or else demagogues will corrupt and exhaust them.

What these insights mean for American democracy is that political, media, and education leaders must unite to keep demagogues out of the presidential pipeline. Democrats and Republicans together should teach the American people that demagogues are the Achilles' heel of democracy. Democrats and Republicans together should solemnly ask the people to unite across political and social divides to keep demagogues out of the highest office in the country, notwithstanding party affiliation.

The enemy of democracy is not a Democrat or Republican. It is a demagogue. This is the singular message the political and media leadership of both parties should promulgate together across the nation in order to sustain and revivify our once great constitutional republic.

I. CAMPAIGN FOR PRESIDENT

I'VE RESISTED USING THE WORD 'DEMAGOGUE' TO DESCRIBE DONALD TRUMP —BUT NOW IT'S CLEAR

Michael Signer

In the 17th century, poet John Milton called it a "goblin word"—a sobriquet so low that it was reserved for only the most insidious of rabble-rousers—yet in the last few months, any number of observers, from GOP presidential also-ran Rick Perry to former Labor Secretary Robert Reich, from *The Economist* to, most recently, *The New York Times*, have crossed a rhetorical line in our politics by calling Donald Trump out as a "demagogue."

Until recently, I've resisted it. As the author of *Demagogue: The Fight to Save Democracy from Its Worst Enemies*, I have been asked countless times in recent years whether Trump is a demagogue, and have always responded—indeed, thought—that he was not. Clearly, though, with his escalating effrontery toward the American creed, he is now.

This is not a matter of mere semantics. In the same way that precision should be used when issuing a terror alert, the term demagogue, properly applied, should be a tocsin of democracy—deployed judiciously and ringing loudly to foretell a singular menace to our republic.

The word dates back to ancient Athens, where the original term in Greek literally meant leader (*agogos*) of the people (*demos*).

In 1838, American author James Fenimore Cooper observed that true demagogues met four criteria: they posture as men of the common people; they trigger waves of powerful emotion; they manipulate this emotion for political benefit; and they threaten or break established principles of governance.

1

I used to give Trump a pass on the first and last of those points. It was a bit difficult to regard someone who's always made such a spectacle of his glitzy skyscrapers and lavish private golf courses as a man of the people. And in the presidential race he seemed, initially, more intent on bringing the parlance of business to governance than on undermining government itself.

But over the last several weeks, Trump has crossed both lines.

Despite his billionaire status, he's fashioned himself into a mirror of the masses by appealing directly to the anxieties of a "silent majority" of mostly working- and middle-class white voters.

And he's come perilously close to sanctioning not only inflammatory language—blithely impugning Latino immigrants and Muslim refugees—but violent behavior, reacting to an incident in which a protester was physically confronted at one of his campaign events by saying, "Maybe he should have been roughed up."

On Sunday's "Meet The Press," he called last Friday's shooting at a Planned Parenthood facility in Colorado Springs "terrible," but at the same time made a point of remarking on what he described as "a lot of anxiety" and "a lot of dislike for Planned Parenthood" among the supporters who attend his rallies.

He's demonstrated a penchant not only for perpetuating falsehoods, but for doubling down on them, such as the canard that he "watched" as "thousands and thousands" of people in Jersey City cheered the 9/11 attacks—bringing maximal heat and minimal light to the public discourse.

Cooper observed, "The demagogue always puts the people before the constitution and the laws, in face of the obvious truth that the people have placed the constitution and the laws before themselves."

And while, so far, Trump has only said he'd "strongly consider" closing certain mosques and briefly flirted with the idea of instituting a registry for Muslims, even entertaining these proposals undermines our shared civic values.

In different times and places, demagogues have used this approach to build loyal, self-contained constituencies accountable to them alone: in ancient Athens, Cleon, the brutal general who helped depose the statesman Pericles; in the Jim Crow South, segregationist governors Eugene Talmadge of Georgia, Theodore Bilbo of Mississippi and George Wallace of Alabama; more recently, Venezuelan President Hugo Chavez's "Capitalism is the way of the devil" refrain now almost sounds like an inverse bookend to Trump's real-estate-tycoon bombast.

Throughout history, when they appear, demagogues have been seen as existential threats to democracy.

In Federalist No. 1, Alexander Hamilton warned of leaders who begin "paying an obsequious court to the people; commencing demagogues, and ending tyrants." At the Constitutional Convention, James Madison argued that only an extended republic could diffuse "the mischievous influence of demagogues."

It was with demagogues in mind that the framers devised a series of constitutional checks and balances, including the United States Senate—which Madison described as a "necessary fence" against "fickleness and passion"—and the Electoral College, whose independent electors could, theoretically, stop a demagogue from becoming president.

But even if he doesn't reach the White House, Trump can still harm the nation in other ways. He already has—by embarrassing the United States on the world stage, dividing Americans against each other and hastening the advent of a "fact-free" presidential campaign.

Just as an autoimmune disease attacks the body through its own defenses, demagogues are a disorder native to democracy itself. It's no surprise, then, that the word has been invoked most profoundly in democracies concerned about their integrity.

In 1935, Americans watched with alarm as the ultimate demagogue, Adolf Hitler, began subverting Weimar Germany's fragile democracy from within by turning Germans against their constitution.

It was no accident that the same year, Sinclair Lewis wrote the best-seller *It Can't Happen Here*, depicting the rise of an American demagogue-cum-tyrant named Buzz Windrip, and Gen. Hugh Johnson pointed to Senator Huey Long and Father Charles Coughlin as societal menaces "preaching not construction, destruction."

The American people understood what they were dealing with then: democracy's enemy within. And we'd be wise to accurately diagnose it now. Trump is a demagogue. Not just in a casual sense, but in the most powerful meaning of the word, and he should be confronted as such.

This essay originally appeared in The Washington Post *on December 2, 2015.*

WHAT WE TALK ABOUT WHEN WE TALK ABOUT 'DEMAGOGUES'

Megan Garber

He's been compared to Hitler. And also Voldemort. And also Mussolini, and an African dictator, and Sanjaya, and Biff Tannen from *Back to the Future*, and, mainly for aesthetic purposes, an orangutan. And yet recently, a new epithet has emerged to describe Donald J. Trump, one that aims in its way to combine all those other comparisons into a single, sweeping dismissal: "demagogue." "Textbook Demagogue." "American Demagogue." "Thug demagogue."

As an insult, certainly—as an implicit invalidation of one's political rhetoric—"demagogue" is a very good word. It's slightly gentler than "fascist" and slightly more dignified than "buffoon"; it's extremely opinionated, and yet carries itself with the gravitas of informed objectivity. Uttered aloud—that evocative agog—it forces one's mouth to gape appropriately. And while Trump is certainly not the only contemporary politician to be dismissed under its auspices ("Demagoguery 101," Charles Krauthammer wrote of President Obama and his policies), no figure has so clearly deserved the word since Huey Long and Joe McCarthy and Pat Buchanan riled the former century. So deep has the impact of Trump's fist-pounding rhetoric been that, at this point, there's a metonymic circularity to the whole thing. *The Economist* recently published an article titled "The Art of the Demagogue." It did not need to clarify who it was about.

But what, actually, are people accusing Trump of when they accuse him of demagoguery? It's not simply Biffery or buffoonery or baboonery; it's something more contextualized. More systemic. More dangerous. To call Trump a "demagogue" is to do two things at once: to dismiss him as a political candidate and amplify him as a political threat. That is appropriate, because the key thing about demagogues, historically, is that they have been people who, by way of their very popularity, threaten the populace. They undermine the stability of a "by the people" form of government particularly by turning "the people" against each other. They represent a danger not just to electoral outcomes or political parties, but to democracy itself.

"Demagogue," as a term—"demos," the people, and "agogos," leader—is pretty much as old as democracy is. It was born, like so many others of our most effective insults, in ancient Athens. And despite its anodyne etymology, it almost instantly took on a negative connotation: In Greece, the demagogue was not just a leader of people, but a leader who led, specifically, by bullying/cajoling/converting charisma into influence. He was a populist who appealed, in particular, to the lower classes. As Aristotle wrote of Cleon, a tanner, "He was the first who shouted on the public platform, who used abusive language and who spoke with his cloak girt around him, while all the others used to speak in proper dress and manner."

Aristotle described Cleon and his fellow platform-shouters as "gadflies," which captured not just how annoying he found them to be, but also how destructive: When large animals are pestered into a frenzy, one thing that can result is a stampede that sends them, collectively, over a cliff. For Aristotle, demagogues—people who used democracy, he felt, against itself—were potential threats to the political system he and his fellow democracy-designers were trying to build. "Revolutions in democracies," he declared, "are generally caused by the intemperance of demagogues."

The Athenian democracy did, in its way, survive. But its philosopher's fear of demagogues, and of the vague threat they suggested of revolution from within, extended into the modern world. It is Charles I, arguing (unsuccessfully) for the monarchy and for his life in Eikon Basilike, who is generally credited with re-introducing the term into English. (Whereupon John Milton, as both an avid republican and perhaps an even more avid inventor of language, dismissed it as a "Goblin word," sniffing: "The King by his leave cannot coine English as he could

Money, to be current.")

But while the word proved its utility as both a political description and an epithet, it also, thus anglicized, lost some of the Aristotelian certainty that had defined it in earlier ages. Latham's *A Dictionary of the English Language*, a reprint of Doctor Johnson's sweeping version from 1755, defines "demagogue" as "ringleader of the rabble" but also, secondarily, as a "popular and factious orator." *A New Dictionary of the English Language*, published in 1867, lists "demagogue" as "a leader of the people," but goes on to suggest that the term is "applied to a factious or seditious leader." Trollope, in his 1855 novel *The Warden*, demurred: "Now I will not say that the archdeacon is strictly correct in stigmatizing John Bold as a demagogue, for I hardly know how extreme must be a man's opinions before he can be justly so called."

That muddled sense of demagoguery—extremity that is threatening both despite and because of its vagueness—continues today. (This despite efforts among academics to classify demagogues: Type I, Type II, and so on.) And it is enabled not just by TV and Twitter and a cultural environment that converts human charisma into mass media, but by our political system itself. As Michael Signer notes in *Demagogue: The Fight to Save America From Its Own Worst Enemies*: "Democracy—and any other system with an element of democracy—intrinsically creates an opening for a demagogue."

Today, perhaps as a response to that vague but ongoing threat of media-driven menace, "demagogue" has become a term of last resort: a description—a deeply loaded epithet—that is summoned only when a particular politician or media figure or other modern people-leader has moved so far away from the mainstream that the Overton Window has receded well into the distance. It's a word that doubles as a siren for a democratic system, directed at one person but implicating us all: Our house is on fire. It's this sense that gave the phrase its shock value, and its lasting power, when H.L. Mencken dismissed Huey Long as "a backwoods demagogue." And when Joe Kennedy decried Father Coughlin as "an out and out demagogue." It is why American history, its terrain so widely populated with people who bluster and flatter and smarm and shout, has anointed so few actual "demagogues."

Which makes it telling, and significant, that the people who today are writing the rough draft of future histories are playing that trump card against one, yes, Donald Trump. You could dismiss those dismissals as misinformed, or melodramatic, or evidence that the Internet's outrage machine has once again overridden nuance and/or rational thought. You could, too, point out the obvious: that there is an extent, inevitably, to which demagoguery is in the eye of the beholder. (Plutarch, in Theseus, wrote of Menestheus, who "sowed disturbance" among the "common people" by "telling them, that though they pleased themselves with the dream of liberty, in fact they were robbed of their country and religion"—a description that might also apply to a freedom fighter, or a revolutionary, or any other person whom history remembers as a "hero.")

You could say, basically, that Trump's popular reception has been making exceedingly clear what every "demagogue" will: that one person's threat to democracy is another person's populist hero.

And yet. Democracy, by its nature, allows for only so much relativism. At a certain point—that point traditionally being an election—the people will have to come to some kind of awkward agreement about who they are and what they want. At some point, too, they will have to decide what Trump is, and whether they can stomach what he claims to represent.

In the meantime, though, Trump embodies, with his pounding fist and his artilleried insults and his cheeky baseball cap, the uneasy compromise of the American experiment. He is a human distillation of the maxim that democracy "is a device that ensures we shall be governed no better than we deserve." In all that, he may well represent just what Aristotle feared: democracy, feeding on itself. And thereby destroying itself. Which is a fear, it's worth noting, shared by the founders. As Alexander Hamilton, summoning his reading of history and human nature, warned: "Of those men who have overturned the liberty of republics, the greatest number have begun their career by playing an obsequious court to the people, commencing demagogues and ending tyrants."

This essay originally appeared in The Atlantic *on December 10, 2015.*

THE RHETORICAL BRILLIANCE OF TRUMP THE DEMAGOGUE

Jennifer Mercieca

Donald Trump's December 7 "Statement on Preventing Muslim Immigration" has attracted worldwide disdain. Nearly 500,000 Britons have signed a petition asking their government to prevent Trump from entering their country. In the US, Trump's comments have been denounced by Democrats, Republicans, the media and religious groups.

Yet a recent poll has found that 37 percent of likely voters across the political spectrum agree with a "temporary ban" on Muslims entering the US.

Trump possesses an arrogance and volatility that makes most voters recoil. So how has he maintained a grip on a segment of the Republican base that – at least, for now – seems unshakable?

And how has his support persisted, despite the fact that some have called him a demagogue and a fascist, or that political observers have found parallels between him and polarizing figures like George Wallace, Joseph McCarthy, Father Coughlin – even Hitler?

As a scholar of American political rhetoric, I write about and teach courses on the use and abuse of rhetorical strategy in public discourse. Scrutinizing Trump's rhetorical skills can partially explain his profound and persistent appeal.

The Greek word "demagogue" (demos = people + agōgos = leader) literally means "a leader of the people." Today, however, it's used to describe a leader who capitalizes on popular prejudices, makes false claims and promises, and uses arguments based on emotion rather than reason.

Donald Trump appeals to voters' fears by depicting a nation in crisis, while positioning himself as the nation's hero – the only one who can conquer our foes, secure our borders and "Make America Great Again."

His lack of specificity about *how* he would accomplish these goals is less relevant than his self-assured, convincing rhetoric. He urges his audiences to "trust him," promises he is "really smart" and flexes his prophetic muscles (like when he claims to have predicted the 9/11 attacks).

Trump's self-congratulating rhetoric makes him appear to be the epitome of hubris, which, according to research, is often the least attractive quality of a potential leader. However, Trump is so consistent in his hubris that it appears authentic: his greatness is America's greatness.

So we can safely call Trump a demagogue. But one fear of having demagogues actually attain real power is that they'll disregard the law or the Constitution. Hitler, of course, is a worst-case example.

Amazingly, one of Trump's very arguments is that he *won't* be controlled. On the campaign trail, he's harnessed his macho businessman persona – crafted through social media and years spent on TV (where he was often the most powerful person in the room) – to make his case for the presidency. It's a persona that rejects restraints: he speaks of not being constrained by his party, media, other candidates, political correctness, facts – anything, really. In a sense, he's fashioning himself as an uncontrollable leader.

But most voters would never want an uncontrollable president. So why do so many remain adamant in their support?

First, Trump draws on the myth of American exceptionalism. He depicts the United States as the world's best hope: there is only one chosen nation and, as president, all of his decisions work toward making America great. By tying himself to American exceptionalism – while classifying his detractors as "weak" or "dummies" – he's able to position his critics as people who don't believe in, or won't contribute to, the "greatness" of the nation.

Trump also uses fallacious and divisive rhetorical techniques that prevent him from being questioned or backed into a corner.

He often uses ad populum arguments, which are appeals to the wisdom of the crowd ("polls show," "we're winning everywhere").

When opponents question his ideas or stances, he'll employ ad hominem attacks – or criticisms of the person, rather than the argument (dismissing his detractors as "dummies," "weak" or "boring"). Perhaps most famously, he derided Carly Fiorina's appearance when she started to go up in the polls after the first Republican debate ("Look at that face!" he cried. "Would anyone vote for that? Can you imagine that, the face of our next president?").

Finally, his speeches are often peppered with ad baculum arguments, which are threats of force ("when people come after me they go down the tubes").

Because demagogues make arguments based on false claims and appeal to emotion, rather than reason, they'll often resort to these devices. For example, during his 1968 presidential run, George Wallace declared, "If any demonstrator ever lays down in front of my car, it'll be the last car he'll ever lay down in front of" (ad baculum). And Senator Joseph McCarthy resorted to an ad hominem attack when he derided former Secretary of State Dean Acheson as a "pompous diplomat in striped pants with a phony British accent."

Trump will also employ a rhetorical technique called paralipsis to make claims that he can't be held accountable for. In paralipsis, the speaker will introduce a topic or argument by saying he doesn't want to talk about it; in truth, he or she *wants* to emphasize that very thing.

For example, in New Hampshire on December 1, he said, "But all of [the other candidates] are weak and they're just weak – I think that they are weak generally if you want to know the truth. But I don't want to say that because I don't want to...I don't want to have any controversies, no controversies, is that okay? So I refuse to say that they are weak generally, okay?"

Let's return to Trump's December 7, 2015, statement about Muslims to analyze which rhetorical techniques are in play:

Without looking at the various polling data, it is obvious to anybody the hatred is beyond comprehension. Where this hatred comes from and why we will have to deter-mine. Until we are able to determine and understand this problem and the dangerous threat it poses, our country cannot be the victims of horrendous attacks by people that believe only in Jihad, and have no sense of reason or respect for human life. If I win the election for President, we are going to Make America Great Again.

In this statement, Trump immediately makes two things axiomatic (or unquestionable): American exceptionalism and Muslims' hatred for America. According to Trump, these axi-oms are supported by the wisdom of the crowd (ad populism); they are "obvious to anybody."

He also defines Muslims in essential terms as people who be-lieve only in jihad, are filled with hatred and have no respect for human life. Trump uses Reification – the treatment of objects as people and people as objects – to link his axioms together and support his case: "Our country cannot be the victims of horrendous attacks by people that believe only in jihad."

Here, he personifies "our country" by presenting the nation as a person. Meanwhile, he uses "that" rather than "who" to sig-nal that Muslims are not people, but objects.

His underlying logic is that our nation is a victim of these "objects." Objects need not be treated with the same amount of care as people. Therefore we are justified in preventing Muslims from entering the country.

Finally, it's worth noting that Trump's use of evidence is in-complete and biased toward his point of view. His announce-ment cites a survey of American Muslims "showing 25 percent of those polled agreed that violence against Americans here in the United States is justified."

The polling data came from the Center for Security Policy (CSP), which the Southern Poverty Law Center has called an "anti-Muslim think tank." Furthermore, Trump fails to re-port that in the same survey, 61 percent of American Muslims agreed that "violence against those that insult the prophet Muhammad, the Qur'an, or Islamic faith" is not acceptable. Nor does he mention that 64 percent didn't think that "violence against Americans here in the United States can be justified as part of the global jihad."

Unfortunately, like a true demagogue, Trump doesn't seem all too concerned with the facts.

This essay originally appeared in The Conversation *on December 11, 2015.*

DEMAGOGUES IN HISTORY: WHY TRUMP EMPHASIZES EMOTION OVER FACTS

Richard Ashby Wilson

You may have heard news media and political rivals describe Donald Trump as a "demagogue" this presidential primary season.

Hillary Clinton used the term to describe Trump in a MSNBC interview:

"That's what a demagogue does: They say whatever they need to say to try to stir up the passions of people."

The term demagogue is conventionally defined as a political leader who tries to get support by making false claims and promises and using arguments based on prejudice and emotion rather than reason.

America has a deep and abiding history of demagogues, including Louisiana's Huey Long, Alabama's George Wallace, and Washington D.C.'s Pat Buchanan.

In my research, I examine the efforts to hold demagogues around the world accountable for spreading violent propaganda. Kenyan Vice President William Ruto and former Vice President of Serbia Vojislav Šešelj, for example, are currently awaiting verdicts in The Hague for allegedly inciting violence against other ethnic groups. Dutch politician Geert Wilders is facing charges of insulting a group of people based on race, and inciting discrimination and hatred.

For better and worse, America is an outlier in its legal tolerance of demagogues who incite ethnic and racial hatred, in large part because of First Amendment jurisprudence after World War I that left political speech to compete in "the marketplace of ideas."

The rhetoric of political persuasion is remarkably the same in different countries and across history.

In speeches, politicians embrace repetition, since even an outright lie gains legitimacy if it is repeated often enough. Politicians adopt unusual speech patterns like ungrammatical phrases and long pauses, that entice their audience to listen more closely.

Populists often conjure vivid images and intense emotions that highlight the sacred security of national boundaries. They often use innuendo to besmirch the reputation of opponents. Some claim divine inspiration for their cause.

Often coming of age in an atmosphere of uncertainty or instability, demagogues are different than garden variety populists.

Demagogues do not reassure the electorate with a rational assessment of risk as mainstream politicians tend to do. Instead, they play up existing threats, embrace a narrative of victimhood and sow despair.

Mocking, humiliating and denigrating scapegoats is their stock in trade. Rwandan radio broadcasters followed this pattern during the 1994 genocide of Tutsis.

Demagogues often seek to instill fear by constantly telling their followers they are under mortal threat. Our research shows that encouraging an audience to take revenge on their adversaries, usually minorities and outsiders, is a particularly effective way to mobilize a base to action.

This is when political demagoguery turns from merely worrying to dangerous.

All successful politicians employ the techniques of populism.

Hillary Clinton has been known to exaggerate and repeat herself. Ted Cruz speaks with operatic pauses and has leaned heavily on religious imagery for his credibility. Bernie Sanders paints a haunting picture of inequality in America and his villain is always big corporations.

Most presidential candidates have suggested unsavory things about their opponents and virtually all of them paint a frightening image of what will happen if they're not elected.

But Donald Trump is the only current presidential candidate who crosses the line from populist to demagogue.

Trump exaggerates his personal wealth and his ability to solve intractable foreign policy problems. He proceeds through innuendo, for instance expressing disgust at Hillary Clinton's bathroom break during the last Democratic debate. Contempt and disgust are also expressed at Mexicans, African-Americans, women, Muslims, and the disabled.

Our research shows that directing moral disgust at a target group unconsciously consolidates the identity of the in-group, his followers, who may as a result feel more empowered and in charge of their destiny.

Donald Trump has not refrained from moral justifications for violence. He wants to bring back "waterboarding" with the logic that "if it doesn't work, they deserve it anyway for what they do to us." When a protester shouted "Black Lives Matter" at a rally in Alabama and was punched, Trump condoned the violence afterwards, saying "Maybe he deserved to get roughed up."

Trump's blanket vilifying of all Muslims is seen by some as condoning the increasing number of hate crimes against Muslim Americans.

Even the ardent defender of free speech John Stuart Mill recognized that defaming a group when there's an angry crowd outside their house constitutes criminal incitement to violence.

For a short time, Huey Long, George Wallace and Pat Buchanan attained prominent positions of political influence as a result of their invective against ethnic minorities. The polls five days before the Iowa Caucus seem to indicate success for Trump too.

But a reliance on whipping up anger and resentment is an unstable, high-risk strategy. Even Niccolo Machiavelli warned in his how-to manual of political deception *The Prince* that "The populace is by nature fickle." Supporters quickly turn against crafty leaders once they realize that they are being manipulated to satisfy the demagogue's own egotistical craving for admiration and power.

Ultimately, the political instability and conflict inherent in the demagogue's tactics precipitates his political downfall. Those who live by chaos ultimately perish by chaos.

Public awareness is key to stopping a demagogue.

A famous study demonstrated that just telling youths that they were about to be persuaded by a speaker made them more skeptical of the message. Laying bare the hackneyed techniques of the demagogue can inoculate listeners against them.

Demagogues are vulnerable because they set up massively unrealistic expectations. Eventually it becomes apparent that their claims lack sound basis. The ability of the media to puncture the bubble is one reason why demagogues despise them so intensely. Perhaps this explains Trump's attacks on Megyn Kelly of Fox News.

At various points in its history, America has learned that scapegoating religious and ethnic minorities is not the best way to cope with uncertainty and challenging times. Rather, facing the future without fear and hatred is the only chance we have of uniting our diverse population and achieving economic inclusion and political stability.

In Trump's case, the likeliest scenario is still one of political self-destruction. Egotism, hubris and a penchant for violence inevitably sow the conditions for the demagogue's own demise.

This essay originally appeared in The Conversation *on January 28, 2016.*

HERE'S WHAT DEMAGOGUES LIKE TRUMP DO TO THEIR COUNTRIES WHEN THEY TAKE POWER

Michael Signer

A few hours after Donald Trump won last week's Nevada caucuses, I woke up in the middle of the night with a bad feeling that, as a country, we were now just a Super Tuesday landslide away from putting Trump on the path to the Republican presidential nomination and, potentially, turning over governance of our republic to a man who fits the textbook four-part definition of a demagogue.

Like others I've discussed in *Demagogue: The Fight to Save Democracy from Its Worst Enemies*, Trump's rise has been one of sheer hubris, overblown promises and an almost effortless seduction that can sweep up even the toughest critics. Consider the normally hard-nosed Republican pollster Frank Luntz, who reported "my legs are shaking" after talking Trump with focus group participants last August.

Last month, Trump boasted that he could shoot someone on Fifth Avenue in Manhattan and still not lose votes. Saturday, Trump was apparently tricked into retweeting a Benito Mussolini quote from Twitter account "@ilduce2016"—set up, apparently, by the website Gawker—and brushed it off by saying of his demagogue forbear that "Mussolini was Mussolini" and that it was a "very good quote."

Demagogues know they're getting away with something so shameless that even they sometimes experience it in the third person: Think of Louisiana governor and U.S. senator Huey Long telling an interviewer: "There are all kinds of demagogues...

Some of them deceive the people in their own interests." Or the ancient Athenian demagogue Cleon, who berated an audience for being "victims of your own pleasure in listening" before telling them, "I am trying to stop you behaving like this."

Indeed. When it comes to Trump, my worry is too many voters won't realize, until it's too late to stop him, the four specific and very real dangers posed when someone like him comes to power.

First, a demagogue imperils his country in the international arena. During the Peloponnesian War, the brutal but charismatic Cleon proposed slaughtering all the male inhabitants of the rebellious island of Mytilene—and it was initially adopted. His plan was reversed at the last minute by a vote of the Athenian assembly, but its consideration meant the end of moderate politics in, and the ultimate decline of, Athens.

In the years after World War I, Mussolini translated his populist nationalism into the belligerent foreign policy of *spazio vitale*, which claimed that Italy had the right and duty to seize territory across the Mediterranean region and presaged Italy's World War II invasions of France, Greece and Albania.

Compare that to Trump's 2011 call for America to impose regime change in Libya, saying, "we should go in, we should stop this guy, which would be very easy and very quick." He has assured us that "torture works." He has promised to use targeted assassination against Islamic State fighters, saying, "you have to take out their families." He advocated a "total and complete" ban on Muslims entering the United States for an unspecified period of time, doing his best to wipe out years of goodwill built with countries like Jordan and Egypt while painting a bigger terrorist bulls-eye on Americans' backs.

He's even bragged that he'd "get along very well with" Russian President Vladimir Putin, the autocrat who took Crimea by force and continues to prop up Syria's despotic President Bashar al-Assad.

A President Trump seems likely to escalate tensions abroad and to create unnecessary and dangerous hostilities, while hollowing out our values so that we are no longer the beacon of the free world. Earlier this month he endorsed torture "much worse" than waterboarding, prompting former CIA director

Michael Hayden last week to suggest that military and intelligence officers might "refuse to act" on Trump's orders. A recipe for chaos.

The second danger is that the demagogue will surround himself with incompetent and dangerous advisers. Huey Long famously recruited political operative Gerald L.K. Smith to help run his populist "Share Our Wealth" campaign. After Long's assassination, Smith became known as one of America's most notorious anti-Semites.

President Richard Nixon, who tried his best to qualify as a demagogue with his Checkers speech and Southern strategy, was aided in his decision-making—en route to resigning in disgrace—with his reliance on incompetent and unscrupulous senior White House aides like H.R. Haldeman and Dwight Chapin, whose primary experience was in advertising rather than policy and government.

Trump has been the GOP frontrunner for months, yet he equivocates on questions about advisers he'd choose. Two weeks ago, on foreign policy, he promised, "I'm going to be announcing a team in about a week that is really a good team." That's a promise he's made, and broken, going back to last fall.

Last year, Trump announced the hiring of Iowa activist Sam Clovis as a "senior policy adviser," promising that he would "tap into [Clovis's] expansive expertise in economics, national security and international relations." And while Clovis was an Air Force colonel and is an economics professor, he's light on proven policy expertise. In an October CNN interview, Clovis balked at questions about Trump's assorted inconsistencies on policy. Meanwhile, Trump's national spokeswoman, Katrina Pierson, wore a bullet necklace during her CNN appearance, suggesting provocation will be a staple of a Trump administration.

The third danger is that the demagogue, who ascends to power by manipulating the passions of his followers, will fall prey to passions of his own. Take former Italian prime minister Silvio Berlusconi, a demagogue who built his television empire peddling sexist representations of women and brought those same values into his administration. He became notorious for his "bunga bunga" parties with teenage prostitutes and was convicted on corruption charges.

Trump's Achilles heel is his narcissism. He bristles at any slight, no matter how small, and is determined to make anyone who threatens his self-regard pay. Just imagine how he'd behave with strong-willed congressional opponents who attack him publicly and challenge his administration's policy agenda.

Fourth, demagogues like Trump threaten dissenters in an effort to silence them. Senator Joseph McCarthy (R-Wis.) used the subpoena powers of an obscure U.S. Senate subcommittee to terrorize Americans he deemed enemies of the state. In *The Origins of Totalitarianism*, Hannah Arendt described how, in both Nazi Germany and Stalinist Russia, demagogue-led thug regimes tolerated only state-approved groupthink while suffocating individual voices and ideas.

Trump regularly encourages his six million-plus Twitter followers to harass his critics. And of a protester at one of his recent rallies, Trump said: "I'd like to punch him in the face." He wants to "open up" libel law to make it easier to cow journalists unfriendly to his cause.

It all bodes ill for our representative democracy and deeply-rooted faith in constitutional principles. Alexander Hamilton warned us, in Federalist No. 85, of his worry about the rise of a "military despotism of a victorious demagogue."

And here we are.

Trump isn't winning based on experience or ideology. Polls show that voters gravitate toward him because he's convinced them he's the candidate who "tells it like it is," when, in fact, he's done just the opposite. On the most important questions about how he'd govern, he's managed to sidestep voters' and journalists' questions. He's said little that suggests he'd hew to constitutional norms. And he's conducted himself in a manner not befitting a leader of the free world. In a vacuum, we're left to assume that he'd govern much like demagogues who've come before.

This essay originally appeared in The Washington Post *on February 19, 2016.*

TRUMP'S RISE IS THE RETURN OF THE DEMAGOGUE

Jill Abramson

The rally in Lowell, Massachusetts, was a classic Donald Trump event: 8,000 people packing the venue to capacity, a crowd still angry over the loss of manufacturing jobs (long ago, Lowell was the center of a vibrant textiles industry) and an influx of immigrants to the area. On this cold day in January, Trump, as always, promised to build his wall. "I'll name it the Trump wall, probably," he said to cheers of "USA, USA."

More than a generation earlier, in 1976, I was in Massachusetts to see and hear another American demagogue make some of the same promises to a fiery, almost all-white crowd. This time the state's anger was stoked by the busing of school children in Boston to achieve racial balance and the economic decline engulfing the city.

The candidate then was George Wallace, the famous segregationist, southern governor running in the Democratic primary. Despite being wounded in an assassination attempt and confined to a wheelchair, Wallace still thundered behind a three-sided barrier of bulletproof glass. The scene creeped me out, and at times, just like at some Trump rallies, it seemed the crowd might get out of hand.

I was not surprised when Wallace carried Boston and came in a respectable third in the primary. Recent polls show Massachusetts falling in line for Trump on Super Tuesday. (In the general election, the state is usually reliably blue, and in 1972 it was the only one won by the ultra-liberal Democratic nominee, George McGovern. After President Nixon became embroiled in Watergate, "Don't blame me, I'm from Massachusetts," became a famous bumper sticker).

Trump's applause lines come right out of the same demagogue's playbook that Wallace used. The definition of the word, with roots in ancient Greece, is a "political leader who seeks support by appealing to popular desires and prejudices rather than by using rational argument."

In the annals of American demagoguery, Trump echoes two other presidential candidates I once covered. At a New Hampshire campaign event, I remember Pat Buchanan in 1992 playing to worries over mass immigration and the low birthrates of white Europeans. His denunciation of the Nafta trade deal parallels one of Trump's stock applause lines about abandoning "trade deals negotiated by hacks." Buchanan's challenge to President George HW Bush in the Republican primaries weakened Bush's chance of re-election.

So, too, did the independent candidacy of billionaire Ross Perot. Like Trump, he ran as an outsider and played to fears that America was losing ground. The leading Republican congressional leader at the time, Robert Michel, said he had "the demagogue's gift for oversimplification." So, obviously, does Trump.

None of the others had the advantage of reality television celebrity or buildings brandishing their names. But I worried every time I heard each of them playing the strongman, offering bromides, and invoking fear that the country was going down the drain. None of them came close to winning their party's nomination, though Perot's independent bid ensured Bill Clinton's election in 1992.

There's been lots of debate in the American press over whether news articles should describe Trump as a demagogue or racist. BuzzFeed, a digital behemoth that is relatively new to news, allows the terms to be used by reporters on their social media posts. Most of the older mainstream newspapers and broadcast outlets, steeped in a culture of "objectivity," don't use such loaded terms.

My own view is there is plenty of evidence that Trump is both. His statements about barring "the bad Muslims," his constant complaints about illegal immigrants committing violent crimes and his hostility to Mexico are all racially and ethnically tinged. His elegies to lost American greatness and promises to restore it meet just about every criterion for demagoguery.

"Trump has succeeded in unleashing an old gene in American politics – the crude tribalism that Richard Hofstadter named the 'paranoid style,'" wrote the *New Yorker*'s Evan Osnos on a perceptive piece about the roots of Trumpism.

Hofstadter was the great historian of the last century whose essay, "The Paranoid Style in American Politics," is once again on many reporters' desks. In moments of disquieting change, Hofstadter wrote, "the quality needed is not a willingness to compromise but the will to fight things out to a finish. Nothing but complete victory will do."

"Trump was born to the part," Osnos concluded.

Asked about Trump in a television interview that aired on Friday, Hillary Clinton, too, decried "the politics of paranoia."

An episode of *The Simpsons*, "Bart to the Future" evoked a dystopian future where a President Trump ended up creating a "generation of ultra-strong supercriminals" who could "function without sleep."

That was in 2000. Sixteen years later, could the dystopian future become true – at least the President Trump part? Who can stop him?

Probably not the GOP voters of Massachusetts, who have elected more Republicans statewide in recent years, including the current governor, Charlie Baker, and former senator Scott Brown, a Tea Party candidate who has endorsed Trump.

Probably not the GOP establishment, either. Ron Kaufman is a Bush Republican. As the state's GOP committeeman, he is part of his party's mainstream. He did not seem convinced that the sky would fall if Trump became the Republican nominee. "Back in 1979, no one thought that crazy old Reagan could win" he told me in an interview this week. "The bottom line is that people overreact. The country is going to elect a GOP president."

This essay originally appeared in The Guardian *on February 29, 2016.*

THE GENEALOGY OF AMERICAN DEMAGOGUERY

Michael A. Cohen

The crowd waited excitedly beneath twelve outsized American flags as country pickers serenaded them with renditions of "The Star-Spangled Banner," "God Bless America," "Yankee Doodle Dandy," and "Dixie."

These ditties were interspersed with cries of "Go back to Africa!" and "White power!" while the omnipresent protesters, primed for their role in the evening's proceedings, chimed in with "Pig! Pig! Pig!" and "Two-four-six-eight, we don't want a Fascist state!"

Outside the arena, shoving matches and fistfights broke out repeatedly as Birchers, Nazis, and Klansmen tussled with Trotskyites, Yippies, and Black Power activists. Confederate battle flags were flown, then wrested away and set aflame to chants of "Burn, baby, burn." Cries of "Sieg Heil!" were matched by chants of "Commie faggots!" Rocks and soda bottles, from both sides, pelted the cops, who were trying, without much success, to keep order.

With the crowd inside at a fever pitch, the guest of honor arrived under the watchful eye of hundreds of police officers. He was greeted by a sound so overwhelming that even the jaded political journalists who had seen and heard it all were momentarily stunned. "It was uncontrolled release of frenzied, pulsating passion that seemed almost more sexual than political. . . . It may have been the loudest, most terrifying sustained human din ever heard in New York," said one reporter. This was the hate-filled equivalent of The Beatles at Shea Stadium.

It might sound like a description of the latest Donald Trump rally. But rather, it describes a remarkably similar political movement that laid the groundwork for Trump's political ascendancy this year: that of George Wallace, the former (and future) Alabama governor, who ran as a third-party candidate in 1968.

On the most surface level, Trump, a billionaire who brags of his business acumen and his wealthy friends, could not be more different from Wallace, who regularly described himself as "a former truck driver married to a dime-store cashier and the son of a dirt farmer."

The parallels are not in the men's personal stories, but rather in the divisive, angry, fearful, anti-elitist, and resentment-laden politics that they used to spark their presidential aspirations. George Wallace won just 13 percent of the popular vote in 1968, but he birthed to this nation the idiomatic language of anti government populism—a language that would be utilized by countless Republican politicians over the next four decades. Trump represents the logical culmination of that rhetorical tradition, but perhaps also its final denouement as a politically effective feature of American politics. Trump and Wallace are two sides of the same coin, but one man represents a beginning and the other the end of the line.

Indeed, the similarities, in both style and substance, between Trump and Wallace are profound.

At a time that the federal government's efforts to expand racial integration were upsetting the foundation of white advantage, Wallace reserved his strongest broadsides for the "theoreticians" and "bureaucrats" with their "federal guidelines" threatening to integrate neighborhoods, desegregate schools, and undermine union seniority. As crime rates escalated across the country, he railed against "pseudo-intellectuals" who excused arson and murder by "saying the killer didn't get any watermelon to eat when he was 10 years old." As social mores changed, he complained about the "hes who look like shes" and said of a group of antiwar protesters who'd laid down in front of President Lyndon Johnson's limousine, "If any demonstrator ever lays down in front of my car, it'll be the last car he'll ever lay down in front of."

Forty-eight years later, Trump has focused his venom on a new set of political targets: the illegal immigrants, "streaming over the border" who he says are rapists and murderers; and the Muslims he wants to ban from entering the United States to protect Americans against potential terrorism.

His toughest critiques, however, are for foreign countries, like Mexico, Japan, and China that, he says, are "ripping America off" and the American politicians, too corrupted, too stupid, and too weak to stand up to them.

Just as Wallace railed against the countries America was "handing out foreign aid" to "while nobody helps us out in Vietnam," Trump complains about America taking care of Germany, Saudi Arabia, South Korea, and Japan—and getting nothing in return.

On Vietnam, Wallace would tell his supporters that the only way to end the conflict there was the use of overwhelming force, kind of like a modern politician who thinks the United States should "bomb the shit" out of its opponents.

Wallace also employed overwhelming force on his critics. "All you need is a good barber!" he yelled at the dozens of hecklers in the crowd. "Why don't you come down here . . . and I'll autograph your sandals!" As inevitable fights broke out at his events, he offered no quarter. "Well, you came for trouble and you got it."

Today, Trump offers a more direct response to his frequent protesters, "I'd like to punch them in the face."

But more than just two era-stretching demagogues with similar political rhetoric, what truly unites Wallace and Trump is their ability to expertly voice the fears, resentments, and anxiety of their supporters.

Trump's backers almost on cue extol their candidate's willingness to "tell it like it is." As one young Trump backer said to me in South Carolina, "He doesn't care. He'll say anything." Another in Las Vegas spoke enthusiastically of the fact that Trump repeats all the things he'd been "yelling at his TV for the last seven years."

Back in 1968, George Wallace's wife, Lurleen, talked about her husband in similar terms, "When he's on 'Meet the Press' they can listen to him and think, 'That's what I would say if I were up there.'"

These were the Americans—and often traditional Democratic voters—who looked at Washington and saw leaders who appeared to be profoundly uninterested in their plight. Wallace spoke the most directly of any of the candidates to their concerns. Indeed, until the nation's unions launched a full-scale effort to highlight Wallace's antilabor record in Alabama, some fall surveys of union members in Rust Belt states showed him polling just slightly behind the Democratic nominee in 1968, Hubert Humphrey.

As the legendary political journalist Teddy White put it, they represented the "ignored, unheard and unlistened to." They constituted both haves and have-nots—those who believed they had been left behind and those who'd made progress into the middle class and didn't want to fall back. These were the Americans most deeply affected not only by rising Black prosperity but also by the growing disorder of urban America.

To be sure, plenty of Wallace voters held deeply prejudiced views of Black Americans (more so than the supporters of any other candidate), but many also viewed racial integration in largely parochial, zero-sum terms, in which one group's gain meant another's loss.

These voters bear remarkable similarity to Trump's modern base of support—overwhelmingly white, not college educated, racially intolerant, hostile toward immigrants, dismissive of social progress, and facing bleak economic prospects.

According to a recent study by the Rand Corporation, Trump enjoys a four-to-one advantage among voters who "strongly agree" that "immigrants threaten American customs and values." He also enjoys a healthy advantage among those who believe "women who complain about harassment cause more problems than they solve."

But the one characteristic Trump supporters share, more broadly than all others, is that they "somewhat" or "strongly agree" that "people like me don't have any say about what the government does."

Just as Wallace spoke to the alienated white lower class voters of 1968, Trump speaks directly to many of the alienated, lower class voters of 2016. And, contrary to their political affiliation, Trump's voters might be Republicans, but they are not necessarily conservatives.

For example, Trump bests his nearest rival, Ted Cruz, among GOP voters who have liberal views on economic issues. He does better with those who "strongly support tax increases for the wealthy," back labor unions, endorse an increase in the minimum wage, and support single-payer health care. The same was true of Wallace supporters in 1968—and of the candidate himself.

Wallace ran as a third-party candidate under the banner of the hastily created American Independent Party. Its platform called for more job training for "all Americans willing and able to seek and hold gainful employment"; more federal monies for transportation, education, and even the space program; a significant increase in Social Security benefits; and more support for health care for the elderly. The civil rights leader Julian Bond would later say, only partially in jest, that Wallace confused him, "because he's a liberal on a great many questions, except race." The crucial distinction, of course, was that Wallace supporters endorsed a generous welfare state, just one that served their needs and not that of Black and brown Americans.

Wallace backers could not be pigeonholed as traditional conservatives. Indeed, the Wallace vote did not represent an anti-big-government ballot in the way that we think of such things today. Rather, it was specifically focused on the fear that the federal government's increased focus on helping Black people took benefits away from whites—kind of like elderly white Americans voting Republican in 2010 because they wanted to keep the government's hands off their Medicare.

That message, albeit in sanitized form, would be adopted by two generations of Republican politicians and would ensure that Wallace's legacy would live on far past his failed candidacy in 1968. Indeed, one could argue that the biggest mistake Republicans make today is embracing the tenets of conservative dogma and straying from the Wallace playbook of harsh rhetoric, combined with a pragmatic, generous approach to policy matters.

Of course, Wallace's political success would be rather limited in 1968. Though he polled in the low teens as late as September, his numbers steadily declined from that point forward. It was a byproduct of his increasingly over-the-top rhetoric, the campaign mayhem that followed him on the trail, and the traditional flight of voters from a third-party candidate who can't win.

For voters who liked Wallace's message but didn't want to throw away their votes, they had another option: the GOP candidate, Richard Nixon, who took many of the same positions as

Wallace but presented them in a way that was less extreme and less off-putting. Nixon might have focused on law and order and used harsh tones, but unlike Wallace, he wasn't suggesting that the best way to stop a riot was to "hit someone on the head."

The anti-elitism, the anti government populism, the cultivation of white resentment and alienation, which Wallace used to great effect, and, of course, the dog-whistle racism would become the rhetorical template for Republican politicians ever since. Wallace won only 10 million votes, but he birthed the GOP's modern political narrative. In that sense, Trump owes much to the foundation Wallace put down nearly five decades ago.

What's most extraordinary about Trump, however, is that he's enjoying his success from inside one of the two major political parties. It's a tribute to the "success" of Republicans in embedding the key tenets of Wallace-ism into their political appeals. As the right's new-media guru Richard Viguerie once put it: "We talked about the sanctity of free enterprise, about the Communist onslaught until we were blue in face. But we didn't start winning majorities in elections until we got down to gut-level issues . . . like busing, abortion, school prayer, and gun control."

The problem, of course, for the GOP is that now they are stuck with it. Trump will likely be the GOP nominee, but by appealing to a narrow subset of Americans, the vast majority of whom are Republicans. His kind of Wallace-esque rhetorical bombast is a losing message in a national campaign. Trump's national polling speaks to this. He remains a deeply unpopular figure among Democrats, among independents, and even a healthy minority of Republicans.

After 1968, Republicans got away with adopting a more palatable and less confrontational version of Wallace's language because there was a critical mass of resentful and angry white voters who could be cultivated to win national elections—and who had been trained by Wallace to hear the GOP's dog whistles. There weren't nearly enough Black, Hispanic, or less angry white voters to push back on it. That's not the case today.

This essay was originally published in The Boston Globe *on March 19, 2016.*

CONSTITUTION WAS WRITTEN TO PREVENT TRUMP'S ELECTION

Andrew Trees

E ach day seems to bring a new reason for Republican leaders to contemplate how they might derail Donald Trump at their convention, along with hand-wringing over whether it would be appropriate to violate the will of the people—or at least the will of most GOP primary voters. But there is one group that would wholeheartedly support party officials: the founding fathers.

The founders were far more worried about a demagogue seizing power than they were about following the voice of the people. Most important, they clearly intended the election of the president to be well-insulated from a direct expression of the popular will. That is why we have the Electoral College, which was designed to temper the sometimes clamorous voice of the people.

Although this has led several times to candidates winning the popular vote but losing the election, most recently in the case of Al Gore in 2000, the founders would not necessarily have had a problem with such a result. They were far more worried about too much democracy than they were about too little democracy.

The reason for this was simple: The founders did not entirely trust the people, who were too likely to be ruled by passion rather than guided by reason.

As James Madison wrote, "It is a misfortune, inseparable from human affairs, that public measures are rarely investigated with that spirit of moderation which is essential to a just estimate of their real tendency to advance or obstruct the public good; and that this spirit is more apt to be diminished than promoted by those occasions which require an unusual exercise of it."

No one would argue that "spirit of moderation" has presided over the Republican nomination contest. Much as Madison and the other founders feared, passion instead of reason is the driving force this election cycle, as the recent violence at political rallies has amply confirmed.

The figure whom the founders most feared was the demagogue, whose inflammatory rhetoric stirred the very passions that the founders hoped to control—a fairly apt description of Trump's campaign to date.

That is one of the main reasons the Constitution contains so many roadblocks to the direct expression of the people's will. Much of Madison's Federalist No. 10 is an outline for how the new republic would control demagogues. Enlarging the size of the nation would help "to refine and enlarge the public views" and make it more difficult for "men of factious tempers, of local prejudices, or of sinister designs" to use "intrigue (to) betray the interests of the people," he wrote.

In other words, many of the checks and balances in the Constitution were put there precisely so that people like Trump would not be able to win an election. Actually, the founders feared men such as Patrick Henry, with his impassioned and persuasive oratory, although I believe they'd have found Henry a virtual Pericles compared with The Donald.

The role of political parties in all of this complicates matters somewhat but would not have changed their overall view. The founders almost universally hated political parties and were distressed when the new republic quickly gave rise to protoparties (true political parties in the way that we think about them did not exist until well into the 19th century).

As Thomas Jefferson wrote, "If I could not go to heaven but with a party, I would not go there at all." For the founders, the problem with a political party was that it went directly against the kind of dispassionate reason they hoped would guide all political debates by requiring men to hew to the party line, regardless of their conscience.

What would the founders have thought of party leaders who undermined their own nominating process to keep a man such as Trump from winning? They would likely have congratulated them for doing what wise statesmen are supposed to do—dampening the passion and allowing reason to rule.

The founders found many ways to bridle the voice of the people to avoid what they saw as the "excesses of democracy," particularly when it came to the office of the presidency. They'd undoubtedly find fault with this election season, but not with Republicans for subverting their own nominating process.

This essay originally appeared in The Times Herald *on March 31, 2016.*

DEMOCRACIES END WHEN THEY ARE TOO DEMOCRATIC

Andrew Sullivan

As this dystopian election campaign has unfolded, my mind keeps being tugged by a passage in Plato's *Republic*. It has unsettled—even surprised—me from the moment I first read it in graduate school. The passage is from the part of the dialogue where Socrates and his friends are talking about the nature of different political systems, how they change over time, and how one can slowly evolve into another. And Socrates seemed pretty clear on one sobering point: that "tyranny is probably established out of no other regime than democracy." What did Plato mean by that? Democracy, for him, I discovered, was a political system of maximal freedom and equality, where every lifestyle is allowed and public offices are filled by a lottery. And the longer a democracy lasted, Plato argued, the more democratic it would become. Its freedoms would multiply; its equality spread. Deference to any sort of authority would wither; tolerance of any kind of inequality would come under intense threat; and multiculturalism and sexual freedom would create a city or a country like "a many-colored cloak decorated in all hues."

This rainbow-flag polity, Plato argues, is, for many people, the fairest of regimes. The freedom in that democracy has to be experienced to be believed—with shame and privilege in particular emerging over time as anathema. But it is inherently unstable. As the authority of elites fades, as Establishment values cede to popular ones, views and identities can become so magnificently diverse as to be mutually uncomprehending. And when all the barriers to equality, formal and informal, have been removed; when everyone is equal; when elites are despised and full license is established to do "whatever one wants," you arrive at what might be called late-stage democracy. There is no kowtowing to authority here, let alone to political experience or expertise.

The very rich come under attack, as inequality becomes increasingly intolerable. Patriarchy is also dismantled: "We almost forgot to mention the extent of the law of equality and of freedom in the relations of women with men and men with women." Family hierarchies are inverted: "A father habituates himself to be like his child and fear his sons, and a son habituates himself to be like his father and to have no shame before or fear of his parents." In classrooms, "as the teacher ... is frightened of the pupils and fawns on them, so the students make light of their teachers." Animals are regarded as equal to humans; the rich mingle freely with the poor in the streets and try to blend in. The foreigner is equal to the citizen.

And it is when a democracy has ripened as fully as this, Plato argues, that a would-be tyrant will often seize his moment.

He is usually of the elite but has a nature in tune with the time—given over to random pleasures and whims, feasting on plenty of food and sex, and reveling in the nonjudgment that is democracy's civil religion. He makes his move by "taking over a particularly obedient mob" and attacking his wealthy peers as corrupt. If not stopped quickly, his appetite for attacking the rich on behalf of the people swells further. He is a traitor to his class—and soon, his elite enemies, shorn of popular legitimacy, find a way to appease him or are forced to flee. Eventually, he stands alone, promising to cut through the paralysis of democratic incoherence. It's as if he were offering the addled, distracted, and self-indulgent citizens a kind of relief from democracy's endless choices and insecurities. He rides a backlash to excess—"too much freedom seems to change into nothing but too much slavery"—and offers himself as the personified answer to the internal conflicts of the democratic mess. He pledges, above all, to take on the increasingly despised elites. And as the people thrill to him as a kind of solution, a democracy willingly, even impetuously, repeals itself.

And so, as I chitchatted over cocktails at a Washington office Christmas party in December, and saw, looming above our heads, the pulsating, angry televised face of Donald Trump on Fox News, I couldn't help but feel a little nausea permeate my stomach. And as I watched frenzied Trump rallies on C-SPAN in the spring, and saw him lay waste to far more qualified political peers in the debates by simply calling them names, the nausea turned to dread. And when he seemed to condone physical violence as a response to political disagreement, alarm bells started to ring in my head. Plato had planted a gnawing worry in my mind a few decades ago about the intrinsic danger of late-democratic life. It was increasingly hard not to see in Plato's vision a murky reflection of our own hyperdemocratic times and in Trump a demagogic, tyrannical character plucked directly out of one of the first books about politics ever written.

Could it be that the Donald has emerged from the populist circuses of pro wrestling and New York City tabloids, via reality television and Twitter, to prove not just Plato but also James Madison right, that democracies "have ever been spectacles of turbulence and contention ... and have in general been as short in their lives as they have been violent in their deaths"? Is he testing democracy's singular weakness—its susceptibility to the demagogue—by blasting through the firewalls we once had in place to prevent such a person from seizing power? Or am I overreacting?

Perhaps. The nausea comes and goes, and there have been days when the news algorithm has actually reassured me that "peak Trump" has arrived. But it hasn't gone away, and neither has Trump. In the wake of his most recent primary triumphs, at a time when he is perilously close to winning enough delegates to grab the Republican nomination outright, I think we must confront this dread and be clear about what this election has already revealed about the fragility of our way of life and the threat late-stage democracy is beginning to pose to itself.

Plato, of course, was not clairvoyant. His analysis of how democracy can turn into tyranny is a complex one more keyed toward ancient societies than our own (and contains more wrinkles and eddies than I can summarize here). His disdain for democratic life was fueled in no small part by the fact that a democracy had executed his mentor, Socrates. And he would,

I think, have been astonished at how American democracy has been able to thrive with unprecedented stability over the last couple of centuries even as it has brought more and more people into its embrace. It remains, in my view, a miracle of constitutional craftsmanship and cultural resilience. There is no place I would rather live. But it is not immortal, nor should we assume it is immune to the forces that have endangered democracy so many times in human history.

Part of American democracy's stability is owed to the fact that the founding fathers had read their Plato. To guard our democracy from the tyranny of the majority and the passions of the mob, they constructed large, hefty barriers between the popular will and the exercise of power. Voting rights were tightly circumscribed. The president and vice-president were not to be popularly elected but selected by an Electoral College, whose representatives were selected by the various states, often through state legislatures. The Senate's structure (with two members from every state) was designed to temper the power of the more populous states, and its term of office (six years, compared with two for the House) was designed to cool and restrain temporary populist passions. The Supreme Court, picked by the president and confirmed by the Senate, was the final bulwark against any democratic furies that might percolate up from the House and threaten the Constitution. This separation of powers was designed precisely to create sturdy firewalls against democratic wildfires.

Over the centuries, however, many of these undemocratic rules have been weakened or abolished. The franchise has been extended far beyond propertied white men. The presidency is now effectively elected through popular vote, with the Electoral College almost always reflecting the national democratic will. And these formal democratic advances were accompanied by informal ones, as the culture of democracy slowly took deeper root. For a very long time, only the elites of the political parties came to select their candidates at their quadrennial conventions, with the vote largely restricted to party officials from the various states (and often decided in, yes, smoke-filled rooms in large hotel suites). Beginning in the early 1900s, however, the parties began experimenting with primaries, and after the chaos of the 1968 Democratic convention, today's far more democratic system became the norm.

Direct democracy didn't just elect Congress and the president anymore; it expanded the notion of who might be qualified for public office. Once, candidates built a career through experience in elected or Cabinet positions or as military commanders; they were effectively selected by peer review. That elitist sorting mechanism has slowly imploded. In 1940, Wendell Willkie, a businessman with no previous political office, won the Republican nomination for president, pledging to keep America out of war and boasting that his personal wealth inoculated him against corruption: "I will be under obligation to nobody except the people." He lost badly to Franklin D. Roosevelt, but nonetheless, since then, nonpolitical candidates have proliferated, from Ross Perot and Jesse Jackson, to Steve Forbes and Herman Cain, to this year's crop of Ben Carson, Carly Fiorina, and, of course, Donald J. Trump. This further widening of our democracy—our increased openness to being led by anyone; indeed, our accelerating preference for outsiders—is now almost complete.

The barriers to the popular will, especially when it comes to choosing our president, are now almost nonexistent. In 2000, George W. Bush lost the popular vote and won the election thanks to Electoral College math and, more egregiously, to a partisan Supreme Court vote. Al Gore's eventual concession spared the nation a constitutional crisis, but the episode generated widespread unease, not just among Democrats. And this year, the delegate system established by our political parties is also under assault. Trump has argued that the candidate with the most votes should get the Republican nomination, regardless of the rules in place. It now looks as if he won't even need to win that argument—that he'll bank enough delegates to secure the nomination uncontested—but he's won it anyway. Fully half of Americans now believe the traditional nominating system is rigged.

Many contend, of course, that American democracy is actually in retreat, close to being destroyed by the vastly more unequal economy of the last quarter-century and the ability of the very rich to purchase political influence. This is Bernie

Sanders's core critique. But the past few presidential elections have demonstrated that, in fact, money from the ultrarich has been mostly a dud. Barack Obama, whose 2008 campaign was propelled by small donors and empowered by the internet, blazed the trail of the modern-day insurrectionist, defeating the prohibitive favorite in the Democratic primary and later his Republican opponent (both pillars of their parties' Establishments and backed by moneyed elites). In 2012, the fund-raising power behind Mitt Romney—avatar of the one percent—failed to dislodge Obama from office. And in this presidential cycle, the breakout candidates of both parties have soared without financial support from the elites. Sanders, who is sustaining his campaign all the way to California on the backs of small donors and large crowds, is, to put it bluntly, a walking refutation of his own argument. Trump, of course, is a largely self-funding billionaire—but like Willkie, he argues that his wealth uniquely enables him to resist the influence of the rich and their lobbyists. Those despairing over the influence of Big Money in American politics must also explain the swift, humiliating demise of Jeb Bush and the struggling Establishment campaign of Hillary Clinton. The evidence suggests that direct democracy, far from being throttled, is actually intensifying its grip on American politics.

None of this is necessarily cause for alarm, even though it would be giving the founding fathers palpitations. The emergence of the first Black president—unimaginable before our more inclusive democracy—is miraculous, a strengthening, rather than weakening, of the system. The days when party machines just fixed things or rigged elections are mercifully done with. The way in which outsider candidates, from Obama to Trump and Sanders, have brought millions of new people into the electoral process is an unmitigated advance. The inclusion of previously excluded voices helps, rather than impedes, our public deliberation. But it is precisely because of the great accomplishments of our democracy that we should be vigilant about its specific, unique vulnerability: its susceptibility, in stressful times, to the appeal of a shameless demagogue.

What the 21st century added to this picture, it's now blindingly obvious, was media democracy—in a truly revolutionary form. If late-stage political democracy has taken two centuries to ripen, the media equivalent took around two decades, swiftly erasing almost any elite moderation or control of our democratic discourse. The process had its origins in partisan talk radio at the end of the past century. The rise of the internet—an event so swift and pervasive its political effect is only now beginning to be understood—further democratized every source of information, dramatically expanded each outlet's readership, and gave everyone a platform. All the old barriers to entry—the cost of print and paper and distribution—crumbled.

So much of this was welcome. I relished it myself in the early aughts, starting a blog and soon reaching as many readers, if not more, as some small magazines do. Fusty old-media institutions, grown fat and lazy, deserved a drubbing. The early independent blogosphere corrected facts, exposed bias, earned scoops. And as the medium matured, and as Facebook and Twitter took hold, everyone became a kind of blogger. In ways no 20th-century journalist would have believed, we all now have our own virtual newspapers on our Facebook newsfeeds and Twitter timelines—picking stories from countless sources and creating a peer-to-peer media almost completely free of editing or interference by elites. This was bound to make politics more fluid. Political organizing—calling a meeting, fomenting a rally to advance a cause—used to be extremely laborious. Now you could bring together a virtual mass movement with a single webpage. It would take you a few seconds.

The web was also uniquely capable of absorbing other forms of media, conflating genres and categories in ways never seen before. The distinction between politics and entertainment became fuzzier; election coverage became even more modeled on sportscasting; your Pornhub jostled right next to your mother's Facebook page. The web's algorithms all but removed any editorial judgment, and the effect soon had cable news abandoning even the pretense of asking "Is this relevant?" or "Do we really need to cover this live?" in the rush toward ratings bonanzas. In the end, all these categories were reduced to one thing: traffic, measured far more accurately than any other medium had ever done before.

And what mainly fuels this is precisely what the founders feared about democratic culture: feeling, emotion, and narcissism, rather than reason, empiricism, and public-spiritedness. Online debates become personal, emotional, and irresolvable almost as soon as they begin. Godwin's Law—it's only a matter of time before a comments section brings up Hitler—is a reflection of the collapse of the reasoned deliberation the founders saw as indispensable to a functioning republic.

Yes, occasional rational points still fly back and forth, but there are dramatically fewer elite arbiters to establish which of those points is actually true or valid or relevant. We have lost authoritative sources for even a common set of facts. And without such common empirical ground, the emotional component of politics becomes inflamed and reason retreats even further. The more emotive the candidate, the more supporters he or she will get.

Politically, we lucked out at first. Obama would never have been nominated for the presidency, let alone elected, if he hadn't harnessed the power of the web and the charisma of his media celebrity. But he was also, paradoxically, a very elite figure, a former state and U.S. senator, a product of Harvard Law School, and, as it turned out, blessed with a preternaturally rational and calm disposition. So he has masked, temporarily, the real risks in the system that his pioneering campaign revealed. Hence many Democrats' frustration with him. Those who saw in his campaign the seeds of revolutionary change, who were drawn to him by their own messianic delusions, came to be bitterly disappointed by his governing moderation and pragmatism.

The climate Obama thrived in, however, was also ripe for far less restrained opportunists. In 2008, Sarah Palin emerged as proof that an ardent Republican, branded as an outsider, tailor-made for reality TV, proud of her own ignorance about the world, and reaching an audience directly through online media, could also triumph in this new era. She was, it turned out, a John the Baptist for the true messiah of conservative populism, waiting patiently and strategically for his time to come.

Trump, we now know, had been considering running for president for decades. Those who didn't see him coming—or kept treating him as a joke—had not yet absorbed the precedents of Obama and Palin or the power of the new wide-open system to change the rules of the political game. Trump was as underrated for all of 2015 as Obama was in 2007—and for the same reasons. He intuitively grasped the vanishing authority of American political and media elites, and he had long fashioned a public persona perfectly attuned to blast past them.

Despite his immense wealth and inherited privilege, Trump had always cultivated a common touch. He did not hide his wealth in the late-20th century—he flaunted it in a way that connected with the masses. He lived the rich man's life most working men dreamed of—endless glamour and women, for example—without sacrificing a way of talking about the world that would not be out of place on the construction sites he regularly toured. His was a cult of democratic aspiration. His 1987 book, *The Art of the Deal*, promised its readers a path to instant success; his appearances on "The Howard Stern Show" cemented his appeal. His friendship with Vince McMahon offered him an early entrée into the world of professional wrestling, with its fusion of sports and fantasy. He was a macho media superstar.

One of the more amazing episodes in Sarah Palin's early political life, in fact, bears this out. She popped up in the Anchorage *Daily News* as "a commercial fisherman from Wasilla" on April 3, 1996. Palin had told her husband she was going to Costco but had sneaked into J.C. Penney in Anchorage to see ... one Ivana Trump, who, in the wake of her divorce, was touting her branded perfume. "We want to see Ivana," Palin told the paper, "because we are so desperate in Alaska for any semblance of glamour and culture."

Trump assiduously cultivated this image and took to reality television as a natural. Each week, for 14 seasons of *The Apprentice*, he would look someone in the eye and tell them, "You're fired!" The conversation most humane bosses fear to have with an employee was something Trump clearly relished, and the cruelty became entertainment. In retrospect, it is clear he was training—both himself and his viewers. If you want to understand why a figure so widely disliked nonetheless powers toward the election as if he were approaching a reality-TV-show finale, look no further. His television tactics, as applied to presidential debates, wiped out rivals used to a different game. And all our reality-TV training has conditioned us to hope he'll win—or at least stay in the game till the final round. In such a shame-free media environment, the assholes often win. In the end, you support them because they're assholes.

In Eric Hoffer's classic 1951 tract, *The True Believer*, he sketches the dynamics of a genuine mass movement. He was thinking of the upheavals in Europe in the first half of the century, but the book remains sobering, especially now. Hoffer's core insight was to locate the source of all truly mass movements in a collective sense of acute frustration. Not despair, or revolt, or resignation—but frustration simmering with rage. Mass movements, he notes (as did Tocqueville centuries before him), rarely arise when oppression or misery is at its worst (say, 2009); they tend to appear when the worst is behind us but the future seems not so much better (say, 2016). It is when a recovery finally gathers speed and some improvement is tangible but not yet widespread that the anger begins to rise. After the suffering of recession or unemployment, and despite hard work with stagnant or dwindling pay, the future stretches ahead with relief just out of reach. When those who helped create the last recession face no consequences but renewed fabulous wealth, the anger reaches a crescendo.

The deeper, long-term reasons for today's rage are not hard to find, although many of us elites have shamefully found ourselves able to ignore them. The jobs available to the working class no longer contain the kind of craftsmanship or satisfaction or meaning that can take the sting out of their low and stagnant wages. The once-familiar avenues for socialization—the church, the union hall, the VFW—have become less vibrant and social isolation more common. Global economic forces have pummeled blue-collar workers more relentlessly than almost any other segment of society, forcing them to compete against hundreds of millions of equally skilled workers throughout the planet. No one asked them in the 1990s if this was the future they wanted. And the impact has been more brutal than many economists predicted. No wonder suicide and mortality rates among the white working poor are spiking dramatically.

"It is usually those whose poverty is relatively recent, the 'new poor,' who throb with the ferment of frustration," Hoffer argues. Fundamentalist religion long provided some emotional support for those left behind (for one thing, it invites practitioners to defy the elites as unholy), but its influence has waned as modernity has penetrated almost everything and the great culture wars of the 1990s and 2000s have ended in a rout. The result has been a more diverse mainstream culture—but also, simultaneously, a subculture that is even more alienated and despised, and ever more infuriated and bloody-minded.

This is an age in which a woman might succeed a Black man as president, but also one in which a member of the white working class has declining options to make a decent living. This is a time when gay people can be married in 50 states, even as working-class families are hanging by a thread. It's a period in which we have become far more aware of the historic injustices that still haunt African-Americans and yet we treat the desperate plight of today's white working class as an afterthought. And so late-stage capitalism is creating a righteous, revolutionary anger that late-stage democracy has precious little ability to moderate or constrain—and has actually helped exacerbate.

For the white working class, having had their morals roundly mocked, their religion deemed primitive, and their economic prospects decimated, now find their very gender and race, indeed the very way they talk about reality, described as a kind of problem for the nation to overcome. This is just one aspect of what Trump has masterfully signaled as "political correctness" run amok, or what might be better described as the newly rigid progressive passion for racial and sexual equality of outcome, rather than the liberal aspiration to mere equality of opportunity.

Much of the newly energized left has come to see the white working class not as allies but primarily as bigots, misogynists, racists, and homophobes, thereby condemning those often at the near-bottom rung of the economy to the bottom rung of the culture as well. A struggling white man in the heartland is now told to "check his privilege" by students at Ivy League colleges. Even if you agree that the privilege exists, it's hard not to empathize with the object of this disdain. These working-class communities, already alienated, hear—how can they not?—the glib and easy dismissals of "white straight men" as the ultimate source of all our woes. They smell the condescension and the broad generalizations about them—all of which would be repellent if directed at racial minorities—and see themselves, in Hoffer's words, "disinherited and injured by an unjust order of things."

And so they wait, and they steam, and they lash out. This was part of the emotional force of the tea party: not just the advancement of racial minorities, gays, and women but the simultaneous demonization of the white working-class world, its culture and way of life. Obama never intended this, but he became a symbol to many of this cultural marginalization. The Black Lives Matter left stoked the fires still further; so did the gay left, for whom the word *magnanimity* seems unknown, even in the wake of stunning successes. And as the tea party swept through Washington in 2010, as its representatives repeatedly held the government budget hostage, threatened the very credit of the U.S., and refused to hold hearings on a Supreme Court nominee, the American political and media Establishment mostly chose to interpret such behavior as something other than unprecedented. But Trump saw what others didn't, just as Hoffer noted: "The frustrated individual and the true believer make better prognosticators than those who have reason to want the preservation of the status quo."

Mass movements, Hoffer argues, are distinguished by a "facility for make-believe … credulity, a readiness to attempt the impossible." What, one wonders, could be more impossible than suddenly vetting every single visitor to the U.S. for traces of Islamic belief? What could be more make-believe than a big, beautiful wall stretching across the entire Mexican border, paid for by the Mexican government? What could be more credulous than arguing that we could pay off our national debt through a global trade war? In a conventional political party, and in a rational political discourse, such ideas would be laughed out of contention, their self-evident impossibility disqualifying them from serious consideration. In the emotional fervor of a democratic mass movement, however, these impossibilities become icons of hope, symbols of a new way of conducting politics. Their very impossibility is their appeal.

But the most powerful engine for such a movement—the thing that gets it off the ground, shapes and solidifies and entrenches it—is always the evocation of hatred. It is, as Hoffer put it, "the most accessible and comprehensive of all unifying elements." And so Trump launched his campaign by calling undocumented Mexican immigrants a population largely of rapists and murderers. He moved on to Muslims, both at home and abroad. He has now added to these enemies—with sly brilliance—the Republican Establishment itself. And what makes Trump uniquely dangerous in the history of American politics—with far broader national appeal than, say, Huey Long or George Wallace—is his response to all three enemies. It's the threat of blunt coercion and dominance.

And so after demonizing most undocumented Mexican immigrants, he then vowed to round up and deport all 11 million of them by force. "They have to go" was the typically blunt phrase he used—and somehow people didn't immediately recognize the monstrous historical echoes. The sheer scale of the police and military operation that this policy would entail boggles the mind. Worse, he emphasized, after the mass murder in San Bernardino, that even the Muslim-Americans you know intimately may turn around and massacre you at any juncture. "There's something going on," he declaimed ominously, giving legitimacy to the most hysterical and ugly of human impulses.

To call this fascism doesn't do justice to fascism. Fascism had, in some measure, an ideology and occasional coherence that Trump utterly lacks. But his movement is clearly fascistic in its demonization of foreigners, its hyping of a threat by a domestic minority (Muslims and Mexicans are the new Jews), its focus on a single supreme leader of what can only be called a cult, and its deep belief in violence and coercion in a democracy that has heretofore relied on debate and persuasion. This is the Weimar aspect of our current moment. Just as the English Civil War ended with a dictatorship under Oliver Cromwell, and the French Revolution gave us Napoleon Bonaparte, and the unstable chaos of Russian democracy yielded to Vladimir Putin, and the most recent burst of Egyptian democracy set the conditions for General el-Sisi's coup, so our paralyzed, emotional hyperdemocracy leads the stumbling, frustrated, angry voter toward the chimerical panacea of Trump.

His response to his third vaunted enemy, the RNC, is also laced with the threat of violence. There will be riots in Cleveland if he doesn't get his way. The RNC will have "a rough time" if it doesn't cooperate. "Paul Ryan, I don't know him well, but I'm sure I'm going to get along great with him," Trump has said. "And if I don't? He's gonna have to pay a big price, okay?" The past month has seen delegates to the Cleveland convention receiving death threats; one of Trump's hatchet men, Roger Stone, has already threatened to publish the hotel rooms of delegates who refuse to vote for Trump.

And what's notable about Trump's supporters is precisely what one would expect from members of a mass movement: their intense loyalty. Trump is their man, however inarticulate they are when explaining why. He's tough, he's real, and they've got his back, especially when he is attacked by all the people they have come to despise: liberal Democrats and traditional Republicans. At rallies, whenever a protester is hauled out, you can almost sense the rising rage of the collective identity venting itself against a lone dissenter and finding a catharsis of sorts in the brute force a mob can inflict on an individual. Trump tells the crowd he'd like to punch a protester in the face or have him carried out on a stretcher. No modern politician who has come this close to the presidency has championed violence in this way. It would be disqualifying if our hyperdemocracy hadn't already abolished disqualifications.

And while a critical element of 20th-century fascism—its organized street violence—is missing, you can begin to see it in embryonic form. The phalanx of bodyguards around Trump grows daily; plainclothes bouncers in the crowds have emerged as pseudo-cops to contain the incipient unrest his candidacy will only continue to provoke; supporters have attacked hecklers with sometimes stunning ferocity. Every time Trump legitimizes potential violence by his supporters by saying it comes from a love of country, he sows the seeds for serious civil unrest.

Trump celebrates torture—the one true love of tyrants everywhere—not because it allegedly produces intelligence but because it has a demonstration effect. At his rallies he has re-counted the mythical acts of one General John J. Pershing when confronted with an alleged outbreak of Islamist terror-ism in the Philippines. Pershing, in Trump's telling, lines up 50 Muslim prisoners, swishes a series of bullets in the corpses of freshly slaughtered pigs, and orders his men to put those bul-lets in their rifles and kill 49 of the captured Muslim men. He spares one captive solely so he can go back and tell his friends. End of the terrorism problem.

In some ways, this story contains all the elements of Trump's core appeal. The vexing problem of tackling jihadist terror? Torture and murder enough terrorists and they will simply go away. The complicated issue of undocumented workers, drawn by jobs many Americans won't take? Deport every single one of them and build a wall to stop the rest. Fuck political correctness. As one of his supporters told an obtuse reporter at a rally when asked if he supported Trump: "Hell yeah! He's no-bullshit. All balls. Fuck you all balls. That's what I'm about." And therein lies the appeal of tyrants from the beginning of time. Fuck you all balls. Irrationality with muscle.

The racial aspect of this is also unmissable. When the ene-my within is Mexican or Muslim, and your ranks are extremely white, you set up a rubric for a racial conflict. And what's truly terrifying about Trump is that he does not seem to shrink from such a prospect; he relishes it.

For, like all tyrants, he is utterly lacking in self-control. Sleeping a handful of hours a night, impulsively tweeting in the early hours, improvising madly on subjects he knows nothing about, Trump rants and raves as he surfs an entirely reactive media landscape. Once again, Plato had his temperament down: A tyrant is a man "not having control of himself [who] attempts to rule others"; a man flooded with fear and love and passion, while having little or no ability to restrain or moderate them; a "real slave to the greatest fawning," a man who "throughout his entire life ... is full of fear, overflowing with convulsions and pains." Sound familiar? Trump is as mercurial and as unpredict-able and as emotional as the daily Twitter stream. And we are contemplating giving him access to the nuclear codes.

Those who believe that Trump's ugly, thuggish populism has

no chance of ever making it to the White House seem to me to be missing this dynamic. Neo-fascist movements do not advance gradually by persuasion; they first transform the terms of the debate, create a new movement based on untrammeled emotion, take over existing institutions, and then ruthlessly exploit events. And so current poll numbers are only reassuring if you ignore the potential impact of sudden, external events— an economic downturn or a terror attack in a major city in the months before November. I have no doubt, for example, that Trump is sincere in his desire to "cut the head off" ISIS, whatever that can possibly mean. But it remains a fact that the interests of ISIS and the Trump campaign are now perfectly aligned. Fear is always the would-be tyrant's greatest ally.

And though Trump's unfavorables are extraordinarily high (around 65 percent), he is already showing signs of changing his tune, pivoting (fitfully) to the more presidential mode he envisages deploying in the general election. I suspect this will, to some fools on the fence, come as a kind of relief, and may open their minds to him once more. Tyrants, like mob bosses, know the value of a smile: Precisely because of the fear he's already generated, you desperately want to believe in his new warmth. It's part of the good-cop-bad-cop routine that will be familiar to anyone who has studied the presidency of Vladimir Putin.

With his appeal to his own base locked up, Trump may well also shift to more moderate stances on social issues like abortion (he already wants to amend the GOP platform to a less draconian position) or gay and even transgender rights. He is consistent in his inconsistency, because, for him, winning is what counts. He has had a real case against Ted Cruz—that the senator has no base outside ideological-conservative quarters and is even less likely to win a general election. More potently, Trump has a worryingly strong argument against Clinton herself—or "crooked Hillary," as he now dubs her.

His proposition is a simple one. Remember James Carville's core question in the 1992 election: Change versus more of the same? That sentiment once elected Clinton's husband; it could also elect her opponent this fall. If you like America as it is, vote Clinton. After all, she has been a member of the American political elite for a quarter-century. Clinton, moreover, has shown no ability to inspire or rally anyone but her longtime loyalists. She is lost in the new media and has struggled to put away a 74-year-old socialist who is barely a member of her party. Her own unfavorables are only 11 points lower than Trump's (far higher than Obama's, John Kerry's, or Al Gore's were at this point in the race), and the more she campaigns, the higher her unfavorables go (including in her own party). She has a Gore problem. The idea of welcoming her into your living room for the next four years can seem, at times, positively masochistic.

It may be that demographics will save us. America is no longer an overwhelmingly white country, and Trump's signature issue—illegal immigration—is the source of his strength but also of his weakness. Nonetheless, it's worth noting how polling models have consistently misread the breadth of his support, especially in these past few weeks; he will likely bend over backward to include minorities in his fall campaign; and those convinced he cannot bring a whole new swath of white voters back into the political process should remember 2004, when Karl Rove helped engineer anti-gay-marriage state constitutional amendments that increased conservative voter turnout. All Trump needs is a sliver of minority votes inspired by the new energy of his campaign and the alleged dominance of the Obama coalition could crack (especially without Obama). Throughout the West these past few years, from France to Britain and Germany, the polls have kept missing the power of right-wing insurgency.

Were Trump to win the White House, the defenses against him would be weak. He would likely bring a GOP majority in the House, and Republicans in the Senate would be subjected to almighty popular fury if they stood in his way. The 4-4 stalemate in the Supreme Court would break in Trump's favor. (In large part, of course, this would be due to the GOP's unprecedented decision to hold a vacancy open "for the people to decide," another massive hyperdemocratic breach in our constitutional defenses.) And if Trump's policies are checked by other branches of government, how might he react? Just look at his response to the rules of the GOP nomination process. He's not interested in rules. And he barely understands the Constitution. In one revealing moment earlier this year, when asked what he would do if the military refused to obey an illegal order to torture a prisoner, Trump simply insisted that the man would obey: "They won't refuse. They're not going to refuse, believe me." He later amended his remark, but it speaks volumes about his approach to power. Dick Cheney gave illegal orders to torture prisoners and coerced White House lawyers to cook up absurd "legal" defenses. Trump would make Cheney's embrace of the dark side and untrammeled executive power look unambitious.

In his 1935 novel, *It Can't Happen Here*, Sinclair Lewis wrote a counterfactual about what would happen if fascism as it was then spreading across Europe were to triumph in America. It's not a good novel, but it remains a resonant one. The imagined American fascist leader—a senator called Buzz Windrip—is a "Professional Common Man ... But he was the Common Man twenty-times-magnified by his oratory, so that while the other Commoners could understand his every purpose, which was exactly the same as their own, they saw him towering among them, and they raised hands to him in worship."

He "was vulgar, almost illiterate, a public liar easily detected, and in his 'ideas' almost idiotic." " 'I know the Press only too well,'" Windrip opines at one point. " 'Almost all editors hide away in spider-dens, men without thought of Family or Public Interest ... plotting how they can put over their lies, and advance their own positions and fill their greedy pocketbooks.' "

He is obsessed with the balance of trade and promises instant economic success: " 'I shall not be content till this country can produce every single thing we need ... We shall have such a balance of trade as will go far to carry out my often-criticized yet completely sound idea of from $3000 to $5000 per year for every single family.'" However fantastical and empty his promises, he nonetheless mesmerizes the party faithful at the nominating convention (held in Cleveland!): "Something in the intensity with which Windrip looked at his audience, looked at all of them, his glance slowly taking them in from the highest-perched seat to the nearest, convinced them that he was talking to each individual, directly and solely; that he wanted to take each of them into his heart; that he was telling them the truths, the imperious and dangerous facts, that had been hidden from them."

And all the elites who stood in his way? Crippled by their own failures, demoralized by their crumbling stature, they first mock and then cave. As one lone journalist laments before the election (he finds himself in a concentration camp afterward): "I've got to keep remembering ... that Windrip is only the lightest cork on the whirlpool. He didn't plot all this thing. With all the justified discontent there is against the smart politicians and the Plush Horses of Plutocracy—oh, if it hadn't been one Windrip, it'd been another ... We had it coming, we Respectables."

And, 81 years later, many of us did. An American elite that has presided over massive and increasing public debt, that failed to prevent 9/11, that chose a disastrous war in the Middle East, that allowed financial markets to nearly destroy the global economy, and that is now so bitterly divided the Congress is effectively moot in a constitutional democracy: "We Respectables" deserve a comeuppance. The vital and valid lesson of the Trump phenomenon is that if the elites cannot govern by compromise, someone outside will eventually try to govern by popular passion and brute force.

But elites still matter in a democracy. They matter not because they are democracy's enemy but because they provide the critical ingredient to save democracy from itself. The political Establishment may be battered and demoralized, deferential to the algorithms of the web and to the monosyllables of a gifted demagogue, but this is not the time to give up on America's near-unique and stabilizing blend of democracy and elite responsibility. The country has endured far harsher times than the present without succumbing to rank demagoguery; it avoided the fascism that destroyed Europe; it has channeled extraordinary outpourings of democratic energy into constitutional order. It seems shocking to argue that we need elites in this democratic age—especially with vast inequalities of wealth and elite failures all around us. But we need them precisely to protect this precious democracy from its own destabilizing excesses.

And so those Democrats who are gleefully predicting a Clinton landslide in November need to both check their complacency and understand that the Trump question really isn't a cause for partisan Schadenfreude anymore. It's much more dangerous than that. Those still backing the demagogue of the left, Bernie Sanders, might want to reflect that their critique of Clinton's experience and expertise—and their facile conflation of that with corruption—is only playing into Trump's hands. That it will fall to Clinton to temper her party's ambitions will be uncomfortable to watch, since her willingness to compromise and equivocate is precisely what many Americans find so distrustful. And yet she may soon be all we have left to counter the threat. She needs to grasp the lethality of her foe, moderate the kind of identity politics that unwittingly empowers him, make an unapologetic case that experience and moderation are not vices, address much more directly the anxieties of the white working class—and Democrats must listen.

More to the point, those Republicans desperately trying to use the long-standing rules of their own nominating process to thwart this monster deserve our passionate support, not our disdain. This is not the moment to remind them that they partly brought this on themselves. This is a moment to offer solidarity, especially as the odds are increasingly stacked against them. Ted Cruz and John Kasich face their decisive battle in Indiana on May 3. But they need to fight on, with any tactic at hand, all the way to the bitter end. The Republican delegates who are trying to protect their party from the whims of an outsider demagogue are, at this moment, doing what they ought to be doing to prevent civil and racial unrest, an international conflict, and a constitutional crisis. These GOP elites have every right to deploy whatever rules or procedural roadblocks they can muster, and they should refuse to be intimidated.

And if they fail in Indiana or Cleveland, as they likely will, they need, quite simply, to disown their party's candidate. They should resist any temptation to loyally back the nominee or to sit this election out. They must take the fight to Trump at every opportunity, unite with Democrats and Independents against him, and be prepared to sacrifice one election in order to save their party and their country.

For Trump is not just a wacky politician of the far right, or a riveting television spectacle, or a Twitter phenom and bizarre working-class hero. He is not just another candidate to be parsed and analyzed by TV pundits in the same breath as all the others. In terms of our liberal democracy and constitutional order, Trump is an extinction-level event. It's long past time we started treating him as such.

This essay originally appeared in New York Magazine *on May 1, 2016*

WHY DO DEMOCRACIES CREATE DEMAGOGUES?

Darryl Paulson

T he drafters of the Declaration of Independence and the Constitution did not trust unfettered democracy. The founders wanted self-government, but they wanted a government where minorities would be heard and protected from the excesses of the majority.

Benjamin Rush, a signer of the Declaration of Independence, described simple democracy as "one of the greatest evils."

Alexander Hamilton wrote that ancient democracies "never possessed one feature of good government. Their very character was tyranny."

James Madison, one of the authors of *The Federalist Papers*, argued that in a pure democracy, "There is nothing to check the inducements to sacrifice the weaker party or an obnoxious individual. Hence it is that such democracies have ever been spectacles of turbulence and contention."

The founders' skepticism about democracy emanated from their reading of the ancient Greeks, among other sources. As Plato handed down, Socrates famously asserted that "tyranny is probably established out of no other regime than democracy." From Plato, the founders learned that the longer democracies last, the more dangerous they become. Certainly, the fact that a democracy called for the execution of the enlightened Socrates was not lost on them.

To protect against direct democracy and tyranny, the founders created a political system that erected barriers between the people and the exercise of power.

Voting rights were limited, and the Constitution provided for the indirect election of the president through the Electoral College. The founders also developed a system dividing powers among the executive, legislative and judicial branches. Each would act as a decisive check on the other.

The legislative branch, which they considered to be the most essential to true representative government, had two chambers with distinct powers. House members, elected by the people to serve two-year terms, constituted the democratic chamber. It reflected the will of the people.

The Senate was distinguished by two features. Each state, regardless of population, elected two senators to protect the interests of the small states, for one thing, from domination by the large ones. Second, the six-year term of the Senate and its election by state legislatures, not the people at large, was designed to be a check on the excess passions of the House.

The framers of the Constitution created these checks and balances on democracy to stop demagogues, a unique type of politician who capitalizes on the fact that hatred is a powerful tool in organizing support and creating mass movements. As Eric Hoffer wrote in his 1951 book *The True Believer*, hatred is "the most accessible and comprehensive of all unifying forces."

Stereotyping combines with hatred to create an "us" versus "them" dynamic. Just as the Nazis stereotyped the Jews, the Klan did the same with Blacks.

Now, Donald Trump, the GOP presumptive presidential nominee, is stereotyping immigrants. He has called for a ban on 1.2 billion Muslims from entering America. He has demonized Mexicans as a crime class.

Trump, like most demagogues, also threatens violence as a form of social control. He has encouraged his supporters to rough up demonstrators and even promised to pay their legal bills. At one rally, he told his supporters, with reference to a protester, "I'd like to punch him in the face."

Mac Stipanivich, a long-time Florida Republican consultant, sent a letter to Republicans urging them to work against Trump. Stipanivich went so far as to call him "a boor, a bully, a carnival barker and an embarrassment. Politically, by intent or instinct, he is a neo-fascist."

As legal scholar Christopher Kutz notes, democracy can be "at the same time both fertile and toxic: fertile as a source of humanitarian values and institutions, but toxic to the very institutions it cultivates."

As the founders feared, democracy has created a candidate for president who is toxic to the political system. Let's hope Americans are wise enough to recognize Trump's tactics and strong enough to defeat him in November.

This essay originally appeared in Florida Politics *on May 8, 2016.*

WHAT IS A DEMAGOGUE?

Frederic C. Rich

Last week *USA Today* called Mr. Trump a "dangerous demagogue." Earlier in the week, the editorial board of the *Los Angeles Times* in its endorsement called him "a thin-skinned demagogue." Dozens of other editorial boards and commentators have used the "D-word." But what exactly does it mean?

Demagoguery is a problem implicit in democracy, an occasional illness, if you will, to which democracies are particularly prone. Democracy gives power to the demos, or people, and from time to time the people fall prey to the illusions peddled by a strongman who manipulates them emotionally with the goal of transcending ordinary political conventions or constitutional limits. We call such a person a "demagogue." Hamilton warned in Federalist No. 1 against leaders who begin "paying an obsequious court to the people; commencing demagogues, and ending tyrants."

The demagogue label is thus highly elastic. The critical question is how to distinguish between a charismatic populist politician and a dangerous demagogue. What is that line and when is it crossed? Among political scientists and historians, there seems to be a consensus that when a politician exhibits each of the following six characteristic behaviors, he or she has crossed the line and can be considered a demagogue:

- *Inflammatory language.* The speech of the demagogue is designed to excite popular passions and foreclose reasoned discussion. As Michael Singer, who wrote a recent study of the demagogue, puts it, "bringing maximal heat and minimal light to the public discourse." Lots of heat, but little light, is an apt description of the Trump stump speech, and certainly fits what we heard coming from the Trump side of the stage at the first debate. *The New York Times* analyzed all 95,000 words uttered by Trump during one week, and concluded: "The most striking hallmark was Mr. Trump's constant repetition of divisive phrases, harsh words and violent imagery."

- *Exploitation of popular prejudice and false belief.* The demagogue appeals to the darker side of human nature, targeting the lowest common denominator in a culture, especially fear, resentment, anger, and hatred for a group of "others." *Washington Post* columnist Michael Gerson argues, "Cynically exploiting fear is an art. And Trump is a Rembrandt of demagoguery." Trump's message is aimed at the darkest corners of the American psyche. By dismissing mutual respect and human dignity as only so much "political correctness," he brought forth an eruption of latent anger, prejudice, hate, and misogyny, and rode this foul wave to the nomination.

- *Intolerance of criticism.* The demagogue lashes out against every slight. Rarely content with simply disagreeing with opponents, he seeks to undermine their legitimacy. The demagogue seeks to silence or eliminate critics. And so we see with Trump, whose "birther" libel was irresistible for its potential to delegitimize President Obama, who wants to change the libel laws in order to silence his media critics, and who could not resist using a presidential debate to pursue a long-standing feud with another celebrity. In the same analysis of a week's worth of Trump talk, the *Times* reported: "Mr. Trump tends to attack a person rather than an idea or a situation, like calling political opponents 'stupid' (at least 30 times), 'horrible' (14 times), 'weak' (13 times) . . . ."

- *Incitement to, or tolerance of, violence.* Even before he embraces actual organized violence, the demagogue typically "green lights" violent acts by his supporters, and titillates his audiences by hints of violence to come. Trump signaled his approval of violence at his rallies ("maybe he should have been roughed up" (about a protester assaulted by Trump supporters), "I'd like to punch him in the face"). His speeches are infused with words "kill," "destroy" and "fight." At an event in Raleigh, Mr. Trump was asked by a 12-year-old girl, "I'm scared—what are you going to do to protect this country?" His reply: "You know what, darling? You're not going to be scared anymore. They're going to be scared."

- *Rejection of normal rules of political conduct.* The demagogue thrills his supporters by bucking the norms of political life. He lies with impudence, validates previously off-limits calumnies against the targeted "other," and declines to follow rules and procedures, accusing the established order of being corrupt. Here Trump provides a textbook model, with a wholly unconventional campaign that violates every prior standard of acceptable political behavior, and repeated accusations that the process is corrupt and "rigged" against him.

- *Belief that the passions of the people justify violation of the Constitution and laws.* Demagogues typically do not understand or accept that in a constitutional democracy, the will of the people is limited by the rule of law. It doesn't matter how many people support closing mosques or registering Muslims, it violates the Constitution and cannot be done.   But Mr. Trump insists that it be done, and justifies it as the will of the people as embodied by him. When challenged that our troops might well refuse to obey an illegal order to kill the families of ISIS fighters, Trump replied: "They won't refuse. They're not going to refuse me. Believe me. . . . If I say do it, they're going to do it."

The rise of a modern American demagogue has been expected for a long time. In 1997 the late philosopher Richard Rorty predicted that eventually "something will crack. The . . . electorate will decide that the system has failed and start looking around for a strongman to vote for . . . One thing that is very likely to happen is that the gains made in the past forty years by Black and brown Americans, and by homosexuals, will be wiped out. Jocular contempt for women will come back into fashion . . . All the resentment which badly educated Americans feel about having their manners dictated to them by college graduates will find an outlet."

As so many thoughtful commentators have noted, many of Trump's most ardent supporters share some genuine grievances and anxieties. And in many ways the system has failed them, and failed us all. But the embrace of a demagogue, no matter how valid the popular resentments that fuel him, always ends badly. Always. At some point, even his most die-hard supporters will realize, as Mark Singer put it, "they've been sold out by a huckster who coveted their votes only for the sake of his colossal self-regard. And that, all along, he had nothing real to offer."

This essay originally appeared in the Frederic C. Rich Blog *on October 3, 2016.*

II. FOUR YEARS IN THE WHITE HOUSE

THE ELECTORAL COLLEGE WAS CREATED TO STOP DEMAGOGUES LIKE TRUMP

Michael Signer

Since Nov. 9, Donald Trump has been described as our "President-elect." But many would be shocked to learn that this term is actually legally meaningless. The Constitution sets out a specific hurdle for Trump to ascend to the presidency. And that will not happen until Dec. 19 when the members of the Electoral College meet in their respective states to vote for the President.

It's these electors who actually hold power under the Constitution to select Donald Trump as president. They should take that responsibility very seriously. They owe it to all Americans to deliberate on their choice in the manner required by the Constitution.

The fact is that the Electoral College was primarily designed to stop a demagogue—a tyrannical mass leader who preys on our prejudices—from becoming President.

Consider what Alexander Hamilton wrote in Federalist No. 68. The Electors were supposed to stop a candidate with "Talents for low intrigue, and the little arts of popularity" from becoming president. The Electors were supposed to be "men most capable of analyzing the qualities adapted to the station, and acting under circumstances favorable to deliberation, and to a judicious combination of all the reasons and inducements which were proper to govern their choice."

They were to "possess the information and discernment requisite to such complicated investigations" as the selection of the President, and they were supposed to "afford as little opportunity as possible to tumult and disorder." They were even supposed to prevent "the desire in foreign powers to gain an improper ascendant in our councils."

Hamilton was talking about demagogues. The word "demagogue" appears in both the first and last Federalist Papers; in Federalist No. 85, for instance, Hamilton worried about the "military despotism of a victorious demagogue."

In my book *Demagogue: The Fight to Save Democracy from Its Worst Enemies*, I define demagogues as meeting four criteria: first, they posture as a mirror of the masses, attacking elites. Second, they trigger great waves of emotion. Third, they use that emotion for political benefit. Fourth, they threaten or break established rules of governance.

Demagogues tend to turn democracy against itself, from within, as we have vividly seen in recent years with the tyrannical Hugo Chavez in Venezuela (who imprisoned political opponents), the corrupt Silvio Berlusconi in Italy (who was convicted for corruption and for sex parties with underage women), and the brutal Alexander Lukashenko in Belarus (who runs a violent, oppressive regime).

For a long time, I believed that Trump was not a demagogue because he didn't mirror the masses and because he didn't threaten governance. But when he began openly posturing as a mirror of the masses and courting unlawfulness and even violence, I concluded that he had, in fact, become a demagogue, which meant that he also crossed the line into a clear constitutional danger zone, according to the founding fathers.

For that reason, the Electoral College was designed to prevent a demagogue from becoming president. It serves two purposes. One of them is to give small states power as well as big states and the cities. The other is to provide a mechanism where intelligent, thoughtful and statesmanlike leaders could deliberate on the winner of the popular vote and, if necessary, choose another candidate who would not put constitutional values and practices at risk.

In other words, the electors are not supposed to rubber-stamp the popular vote. They're supposed to do the opposite—to take their responsibility gravely, to subject the winning popular vote candidate to exhaustive scrutiny, and, if the candidate does not meet Hamilton's standards, to elect an alternative.

There is much for them to examine with Donald Trump. In his campaign and in his rocky and unsettling transition so far, Trump has run roughshod over fundamental Constitutional principles.

For instance, he sanctioned violence at his rallies and threatened to imprison his opponent. He threatened the independent press with libel actions and has barred the press from covering him. He has said he would force generals to comply with unlawful orders (for instance, regarding torture) and has threatened to abrogate alliances with treaty partners. And he has done all of these things while stoking prejudices, rage and fear in a way paralleled in our history only by other inarguable demagogues. And his transition so far has been an unsettling parade of erratic and autocratic decisions.

Electors are chosen by their respective state political parties. Twenty-nine states and the District of Columbia have laws in place requiring their electors to vote for the winner of the state's popular vote. But those laws usually impose just small penalties, and Harvard law professor Lawrence Tribe has said that even those fines are constitutionally suspect and may not be enforced by a court.

Because of these rules, the Electoral College has fallen into irrelevancy. This year's election, in particular, the candidacy of Donald Trump, provides them with every reason to perform their job in accordance with Federalist 68.

There are several reasons to think that a revolt against Trump could take place among Republican electors. There's the fact that Trump ran against the Republican Party and their leaders, viciously attacking many respected national leaders. There's the fact that he was unable to win the popular vote—at most recent count over a million votes behind Hillary Clinton.

And then there's the fact that Trump promises to bring to the presidency precisely the "tumult and disorder" that Hamilton warned against.

The electors were supposed to be statesmen. Even though recent years have seen a decline in statesmanship in America, they could be reborn this year. Statesmen truly have our greater good truly at heart, pursuing the broader purpose of America and calming the passions.

If these men and women live up to that noble goal on Dec. 19, they will truly make American great again.

This essay originally appeared in Time *on November 17, 2016.*

YES, TRUMP IS UNDIGNIFIED. DEMAGOGUES HAVE TO BE

Michael Signer

P resident Trump's crude performance last week at an annual gathering of conservatives—he physically embraced the American flag, called the Mueller probe "bullshit" and referred to Representative Adam Schiff as "shifty"—was an affront to the decorum we expect from presidents, and plenty of critics pointed this out. Trump was "not merely undignified as a leader; he is committed to stripping away the dignity possessed by others," Michael Gerson wrote in *The Washington Post*. One Twitter commenter described the speech as "an undignified mess of slop," and another labeled Trump "the most undignified President in history."

But this was the same Trump who as a presidential candidate referred to the size of his manhood during a Republican debate. He said about protesters at his campaign events, "In the good old days, this doesn't happen, because they used to treat them very, very rough." He asserted that "Islam hates us" and that Mexicans are "rapists." Not only did he get away with those offenses, but they somehow made him stronger. And he's gone even further as president. After each episode, Trump's critics have been as scandalized as they have been ineffective, just as they were after the speech at last weekend's Conservative Political Action Conference. During the campaign, Senator Marco Rubio (R-Fla.) called Trump "the most vulgar person to ever aspire to the presidency," and see how far that got Rubio.

In fact, demagogues like Trump are almost always undignified. That is a feature, not a bug, of their politics. When Hillary Clinton infamously described his supporters as a "basket of deplorables," Trump swiftly converted the comment into a badge of honor. It turned out that he wanted his followers to trumpet themselves as "Les Deplorables"—because that was already his argument. While their critics think demagogues hurt themselves politically by violating the standards of polite society, they're doing the opposite: They're doubling down on an unorthodox but potent politics.

In other words, we must understand why Trump's CPAC performance was rational from his perspective before we can begin to understand how to deal with it. And that means taking Trump, his supporters and his "undignified" performances seriously.

A textbook demagogue meets four tests. First, he identifies as a man of the masses, usually by attacking elites. Second, he creates great waves of passion. Third, he uses that passion for political benefit. Fourth, he tests or breaks established rules of governance. Taken together, this approach enables the demagogue to create a state within a state—a massive cult—that follows him alone.

Trump is the first demagogue to actually become president, but American history has seen a lot of them, whether the segregationist Alabama governor George Wallace, the Wisconsin senator and communist-chaser Joseph McCarthy, the Louisiana governor and senator Huey Long, or the Detroit "radio priest" Father Charles Coughlin. World history has seen Mussolini and Hitler and, more recently, Hugo Chávez in Venezuela and Alexander Lukashenko in Belarus.

All of these figures were called undignified by critics who thought their antics could not succeed because they should not succeed. For Chávez, for instance, vulgar language and insults were a trademark, not a flaw. He talked to national audiences about having sex with his wife, called Americans an obscene term, described his bowel movements on television and named the first cellphone made in Venezuela after a popular slang term for penis. Opponents said his talk was crude and made them ashamed. In 2009, a 70-year-old Venezuelan social worker lamented to a reporter, "A president needs to project a good image." But Chavez's power only grew. Only cancer stopped his political career.

Whether you call it decency or decorum or dignity, these old-fashioned standards provide cold comfort when they are the very things demagogues want to blow up as they seek domination. The fact is that demagogues thrive at the lowest common denominator. That is why they relish their status as political bad boys, vulgarians who say things they really shouldn't. That "Oh, no he didn't" sense of daring lets them play the hero in a drama in which they take on the naysaying establishment.

This renegade behavior easily satisfies the demagogue's four tests: attacking elites, stirring massive emotional power, converting that emotion into politics and, most important, obliterating the rules that allow normal governance. Put another way, what so many critics of demagogues have trouble getting their minds around is also the most necessary to understanding them: It's rational for a demagogue to seem irrational.

What I saw last weekend was Trump methodically, over a period of two hours, intensifying his support among his base through a series of precise inflammations, while carefully steering his audience toward the new norms and institutions he's creating. It's the same as when he delights in leading his supporters to angrily chant, "CNN sucks!" The United Nations' human rights chief called those attacks on the press "close to incitement to violence." The accused Florida mail bomber was at one of those Trump rallies, holding up one of those signs.

Most normal people would assume that vulgar, crude people would fail in politics. So how do they succeed, practically speaking? In the ancient world, they were still fairly new, so philosophers were interested in studying them. Aristotle observed that it was easier for demagogues than statesmen to use enthymemes—proofs or analogies dependent on collective past experience—because they shared more in common with the people they were addressing. While educated speakers used "commonplaces and generalities," Aristotle observed, demagogues "speak of what they know and of what more nearly concerns the audience."

What Trump understands is that millions of Americans feel left behind by our politics. They are frustrated by everything about conventional politics, including the expectation that traditional rules like decency and dignified behavior will help solve their problems. They are ripe for a demagogue.

The problem of how elite critics miss the demagogue's strategy, hiding in plain sight, is as old as democracy itself. In ancient Athens, the well-born playwright Aristophanes attempted to undermine a demagogue named Cleon through a series of satirical plays, staged before thousands. Cleon was a colorful figure who said, "As a general rule states are better governed by the man in the street than by intellectuals." After a generation of statesmanlike leaders, Cleon took joy in demolishing decorum. While making speeches, he would do things like suddenly shout, dramatically throw open his tunic and slap his thighs for emphasis. So Trump was following an old playbook when he wrapped his body around an American flag—or when he mimicked a disabled reporter during the presidential campaign. For his followers, these antics are intoxicating.

Aristophanes depicted Cleon in his plays as a vulgar sausage-seller. He mocked the "pig's education he has had." He wrote, "You possess all the attributes of a demagogue: a screeching, horrible voice; a perverse, cross-grained nature; and the language of the market-place." None of this worked. Athenians continued to elect Cleon as general. The plays may have heightened his celebrity.

This pattern has also played out in American history. Consider how the ruling class mocked Long, the folksy Louisiana governor, as he rose to the U.S. Senate. H.L. Mencken dismissed him as a "backwoods demagogue of the oldest and most familiar model—impudent, blackguardly, and infinitely prehensile." In 1931, the new senator cheerfully greeted a visiting German naval commander in a pair of green silk pajamas and a bathrobe. After the German consul's office issued statements of outrage and protest, Long met the commander the next day in a formal striped suit and tails. Long's antics created a sensation of nationalistic defiance, and one historian wrote that Long learned the "value of buffoonery in winning national publicity" and would continue to "cultivate a reputation as a country bumpkin and a clown."

This "bumpkin" was also described by a woman in 1935 as an "angel sent by God." Before he was assassinated by the son-in-law of a political rival in 1935, Long created hundreds of nationwide chapters of his Share Our Wealth Society. He very well could have defeated Franklin Delano Roosevelt in the 1936 Democratic primary for president.

Chávez, too, adopted tactics that were so outrageous, so unthinkable, that they seemed impossible just up until the moment they became successful. As president, Chávez became so audacious in his demagoguery that he made a speech that was literally 10 hours long. But there was method to his madness. He was taking over the state, in plain view.

Demagogues have been with democracy from the beginning. It's not overstating things to say the demagogue represents the battle between darkness and light—between our prejudices and our reason—that's at the heart of democracy itself. After all, Alexander Hamilton worried in the very first of *The Federalist Papers* about those who would pay "obsequious court to the people; commencing demagogues, and ending tyrants."

In his CPAC speech, Trump told the crowd: "I'm in love, and you're in love, we're all in love together. ... There's so much love in this room, it's easy to talk." Faced with the threats of impeachment from Congress and evidence of lawbreaking in the Mueller report, he wants his supporters to choose sides.

As Democratic presidential candidates debate whether to "go low" or "go high" in countering Trump, I'm not one who believes in mirroring Trump's indignities. That won't work for any non-demagogue. After their ruinous experience with demagogues like Cleon, Athenians ultimately addressed the reign of demagogues not through plays but through constitutional punishments. Under a system enacted several years after Cleon's death, a politician charged with "having proposed a measure contrary to democratic principles and to Athens' laws" could be ostracized by a majority of the voters for 10 years.

It's not a far leap to "high crimes and misdemeanors."

This essay originally appeared in The Washington Post *on March 8, 2019.*

WHY DEMAGOGUES WERE THE FOUNDING FATHERS' GREATEST FEAR

Eli Merritt

There has been much talk lately among both Democrats and Republicans of the intents of the founders in the writing of the Constitution, especially involving the powers of impeachment and removal from office.

What has been sorely lacking from this conversation is an awareness of the framers' overwhelming conviction that there was nothing more poisonous to constitutional democracies than demagogues—which to them meant a very specific kind of threat.

Less than two weeks after the start of the Constitutional Convention in Philadelphia, George Washington wrote to his friend, the Marquis de Lafayette, on June 6, 1787, explaining that his critical purpose in attending the convention was to prevent a demagogue from gaining power in the politically unstable young nation and thus destroying it.

Washington described how he was pulled out of retirement by an urgent risk to the United States. "Anarchy and confusion" were threatening the security of the American people and the rule of constitutional law. But this was only half the danger.

The deeper risk, he wrote that early June, was that the political chaos created fertile ground for exploitation "by some aspiring demagogue who will not consult the interest of his country so much as his own ambitious views."

In a letter written three weeks later to David Stuart, a Virginia politician and distant family relation, Washington lamented that the widespread denigration of the Articles of Confederation, and the federal government it created, had rendered "the situation of this great country weak, inefficient and disgraceful." He concluded the letter to Stuart by again stating that the political crisis made possible demagogues who pose a dire threat to the United States.

Washington's greatest fear that summer of decision in Philadelphia was that unwise, self-seeking politicians—even if fairly elected to public office—would tear down the central government and its constitutional laws for the sake of their own advancement and glorification.

Washington, like his peers, did not use the word "demagogue" as an insult or epithet. He did not employ it as ammunition against those he identified as his political opponents. For the steady, rational Washington, "demagogue" was a forensic term that described a well-known class of political actors, known since Greek and Roman times, who obtain power through emotional appeals to prejudice, distrust and fear.

Irrespective of party affiliation, demagogues were a distinct personality type that knew no bounds of politics except fiery self-aggrandizement.

Washington, of course, was not the only framer who viewed our Constitution largely as a bulwark against demagogues. In the surviving records of the speeches given at the Constitutional Convention, the word "demagogue" was used 21 times by the framers as they crafted the Constitution's essential checks and balances against despotism and tyranny.

"Demagogues are the great pests of our government," said Elbridge Gerry of Massachusetts during the convention, "and have occasioned most of our distresses." Gerry further described demagogues as "pretended patriots," unprincipled politicians who steer the people toward "baneful measures" through "false reports."

James Madison of Virginia twice alluded to "the danger of demagogues." Alexander Hamilton of New York spoke of this peril of democracy more than any other delegate, naming it seven times. Demagogues, Hamilton said on the floor of Independence Hall in late June 1787, "hate the controul of the Genl. Government."

Later, Hamilton went on to predict an ominous decline in republics from demagoguery to tyranny. As he put it in Federalist

No. 1: "History will teach us that ... of those men who have overturned the liberties of republics, the greatest number have begun their career by paying an obsequious court to the people; commencing demagogues, and ending tyrants."

Other framers who raised the red flag of demagoguery during the Constitutional Convention were Gouverneur Morris of Pennsylvania, Pierce Butler of South Carolina, and Edmund Randolph and George Mason of Virginia. Mason declared outright that "the mischievous influence of demagogues" was one of the top two "evils" that can befall republican forms of government.

This destructive risk of demagogues is one reason the 55 framers of the Constitution adopted the power of impeachment during the historic convention of 1787.

They believed uniformly that some men, though elected by the people, would be temperamentally incapable of serving the public interest under the Constitution. Therefore, they offered Congress the remedy of impeachment and removal from office.

The framers did not view the exercise of this remedy to be an anti-democratic act of nullifying elections. To the contrary, they provided the people and their representatives with these emergency powers for the specific purpose of rescuing our democracy and Constitution from harm and destruction at the hands of demagogues.

This essay originally appeared in The Los Angeles Times *on December 26, 2019.*

ALEXANDER HAMILTON WOULD HAVE LED THE CHARGE TO OUST DONALD TRUMP

Eli Merritt

I t's not surprising that Representative Adam B. Schiff's opening statement in President Trump's Senate impeachment trial began with an impassioned warning by Alexander Hamilton about the danger of demagogues subverting the Constitution and pursuing personal gain.

"When a man unprincipled in private life, desperate in his fortune, bold in his temper, possessed of considerable talents," Schiff quoted Hamilton, "having the advantage of military habits—despotic in his ordinary demeanor—known to have scoffed in private at the principles of liberty—when such a man is seen to mount the hobbyhorse of popularity—to join in the cry of danger to liberty—to take every opportunity of embarrassing the General Government and bringing it under suspicion—to flatter and fall in with all the nonsense of the zealots of the day—it may justly be suspected that his object is to throw things into confusion that he may 'ride the storm and direct the whirlwind.'"

Schiff (D-Burbank) went on to say that Trump "has acted precisely as Hamilton and his contemporaries had feared"—and that impeachment is one of the core constitutional mechanisms the founders devised to protect our free system of government from such harm.

Now as the Senate sits in judgment of Trump, the members of that body must weigh the prospect of removing him from office—in the face of mounting evidence and testimony—against their own policy preferences.

In this respect, there's a parallel to Hamilton and the Federalists who were tested by the irregular outcome of the presidential election of 1800. In a critical vote in a single chamber of the Congress, they, too, had to choose between preserving the United States' constitutional government and supporting a man who might deliver policies they liked better.

Most revealing of Hamilton's view of the perils of a demagogue in the White House is the stance he took in December 1800 when a fellow New Yorker, Aaron Burr, tied Thomas Jefferson 73-73 in the electoral college vote for the presidency. Hamilton was a Federalist, who advocated for an energetic central government. Jefferson and Burr were Democratic-Republicans, far more concerned with protecting states and citizens from the potential abuses of federal power.

This electoral standoff was unprecedented, driving the selection of the third president into the House of Representatives as laid out in Article II, Section 1, of the Constitution.

Initially, a large group of Federalists in the House wanted to put Burr in the White House, because he was a shaky and capricious adherent to the Democratic-Republican Party compared with Jefferson, who staunchly opposed the Federalist platform of expansive federal powers, broad national taxes, the funded debt, a central bank, and a standing army and navy.

The Federalists in the House, who had it in their power that winter of 1800-1801 to determine the fate of the presidency, considered Jefferson to be their worst nightmare. They deplored his principles and policies on almost every political issue that had emerged since he became secretary of State in 1790. Burr, they felt sure, would bend to their will far more easily, enabling them to advance their party's agenda in spite of his formal affiliation with the Democratic-Republicans.

Hamilton, an acknowledged leader of the Federalist Party, had a radically different view of the impending vote. Burr, a man he knew well from New York political and legal circles, he said, was "deficient in honesty" and "one of the most unprincipled men in the UStates."

One example Hamilton gave of Burr's corrupt intentions in government was Burr's lobbying in New York on behalf of a land speculating company, the Holland Company, while "a member of our legislature."

If Burr gained the White House, Hamilton believed, he would "disturb our institutions" and "disgrace our Country abroad." He would "listen to no monitor but his ambition" and be governed by a singular principle—"to get power by any means and to keep it by all means."

Consequently, when Hamilton heard reports of the Jefferson-Burr electoral tie, he barraged his fellow Federalists in Washington with more than a dozen letters imploring them to "preserve the Country!"

He told them repeatedly that their party must vote for Jefferson, who, though their political enemy and the champion of policies abhorrent to them, was nevertheless a man devoted to the Constitution.

As Hamilton wrote in one letter: "[If] there be [a man] in the world I ought to hate, it is Jefferson." But Burr, he said, would drive the country toward chaos and tyranny, "content with nothing short of permanent power in his own hands."

In a striking echo to the impeachment charges against Trump, Hamilton further noted that if Burr ever reached the White House, there was a risk that, for the purpose of self-benefit, he would undertake "a bargain and sale with some foreign power, or combinations with public agents in projects of gain by means of the public monies."

The historical consensus is Hamilton's efforts that winter to avert a Burr presidency proved decisive. In February 1801, the House cast 35 consecutive ballots for president, none of which achieved the nine-state majority necessary to declare a victor. Only on the 36th ballot, thanks to the votes and abstentions of the Federalists, did Jefferson win with a 10-state majority. Three years later, in a battle of honor, Burr killed Hamilton in a duel.

In Trump's impeachment trial, senators are facing an existential choice similar to what the Federalists confronted in their critical vote: whether to put aside their partisan and short-term policy objectives in the best interests of the nation.

Hamilton's advice today would be the same as it was in the Jefferson-Burr contest of 1801. "The public good," Hamilton wrote to another Federalist congressman as he labored to keep

Burr out of the White House, "must be paramount to every private consideration."

This essay originally appeared in The Los Angeles Times *on January 20, 2020.*

TRUMP IS A CLASSIC DEMAGOGUE: HERE'S WHY THAT MATTERS

Michael Austin

Demagoguery is the special problem of democracy. Both words come from the same root, demos, or "the people." Democracy, or dēmokratía, means "rule of the people." Demagogue, or dēmagōgos, means "leader of the people." And therein lies the problem: in a democracy, where the people have the ultimate sovereign power, they are supposed to be their own leaders.

But having power also means having the ability to give that power away. This is the design flaw in the whole system. If "We the People" have the power to do anything we want, we can give that power away to someone else—someone who flatters us and tells us what we want to hear. Those who flatter kings are called "courtiers," and they owe their livelihoods to the quality of their sycophancy. Demagogues are much the same, but they have to spread their sycophancy much thinner. They have to flatter the people.

But not all the people. Democracy is not really the rule of the people. It is a rule of a portion of the people—those who choose to vote, or those who are permitted to vote. And not even all of them. Just a majority (even if only a procedural/electoral one), no matter how small. Demagogues win by flattering a portion of the people—and by telling them that they are better than another portion of the people. Demagogues have to create and exacerbate divisions. They have to pit us against each other; it is the only way they can win.

And the victories of demagogues come at the expense of democracy itself. Demagogues like Cleon and Alcibiades nearly destroyed the Athenian democracy by plunging it deeper and deeper into the Peloponnesian War. The demagogue Julius Caesar destroyed the Roman Republic and replaced it with an empire. In the 20th century, demagogues such as Benito Mussolini and Adolph Hitler were elected democratically before destroying the democracies that gave them power. And contemporary demagogues have been responsible for much of the democratic backsliding that has occurred in the 21st century, including Vladimir Putin in Russia, Hugo Chavez in Venezuela, Recep Erdoğan in Turkey, and Viktor Orbán in Hungary.

And Donald Trump in the United States. Trump is the textbook demagogue, a latter-day Creon straight from central casting. Those whom he does not flatter cannot understand his appeal. But the portion of the *demos* that he pays nearly all of his attention to understand it very well. He is with them, he accepts them, and he believes the things that they believe that nobody in power has ever believed before.

When historians look for the moment that Trump's presidency became possible, if not inevitable, they will probably settle on April of 2011, when President Obama released the long-term birth certificate that Trump had been demanding for months. Rather than backing down, Trump stuck to his guns and said he was not satisfied, that Obama still had not proven himself a citizen of the United States. At this moment, Trump communicated three important things to the segment of Americans that would be responsible for his 2016 victory: 1) that he believed something that they believed; 2) that he would not change that belief when presented with actual evidence; and 3) that he was willing to endure the scorn of the hated elites on order to stand with them. This is what it looks like when a demagogue flatters the people.

America's founders also understood the demagogue problem very well and took great pains to address it in the Constitution. *The Federalist Papers* begin with Hamilton's observation that "of those men who have overturned the liberties of republics, the greatest number have begun their career by paying an obsequious court to the people; commencing demagogues, and ending Tyrants." Hamilton was not just mentioning demagoguery in passing. One of the primary purposes of *The Federalist Papers* was to show how the Constitution would prevent the emergence of a democratically elected dictator.

But the clearest and best description of demagoguery in America comes from a brief essay by the American frontier writer James Fenimore Cooper—the author of *The Leatherstocking Tales* (*The Deerslayer*, *The Last of the Mohicans*, etc.) who, in 1838, wrote a collection of political essays called *The American Democrat*. One of these essays, called simply "On Demagogues," lays out a set of clear characteristics by which Americans, should they ever need to, could recognize a demagogue:

- *"The peculiar office of a demagogue is to advance his own interests, by affecting a deep devotion to the interests of the people."* Demagogues invariably present themselves as the voice of the people, maintaining the fiction that "the people" speak in a united voice and are universally opposed to the voices of "the elites." In American usage, "the people" usually become either "the American people" or "We the People," while the enemy becomes (depending on the demagogue's political base) something like "the media elite," "the Wall Street elite," "the Hollywood elite," "liberal academics," "wealthy industrialists," or "the one-percent." In the rhetoric of the demagogue, these elites don't count as "the people." They are the "not people" who frustrate the legitimate desires the actual people. And if these elites could just be made to disappear, the real people could govern themselves. (And most demagogues eventually get around to trying to make them disappear).
- *"The man who is constantly telling the people that they are unerring in judgment . . . is a demagogue."* The essence of flattery is telling people that they are right. The essence of civic flattery is telling the people that they are right, that whatever challenges they face are somebody else's fault, and that they do not have to change the way they think or act in order to have successful lives and good government. This sounds like a natural thing for politicians to do, and indeed it is. But it can have severe consequences, since it leads populations

to scapegoat the people whom the demagogue identifies as the ones who are "really" to blame for a nation's problems.

- *"The demagogue always puts the people before the Constitution and the laws."* The difference between democracy and majoritarian tyranny is that a democracy has a system of laws, checks, balances, and safeguards that we collectively call "the rule of law." A major purpose of the rule of law in a democracy is to set up guardrails that prevent the emergence of demagogues. When would-be demagogues are checked by these mechanisms—court decisions, legislative vetoes, Constitutional requirements—they invariably call them "undemocratic." They argue that, because they were elected by "the people," their decisions should have precedence over "unelected judges" or "old-fashioned legislative rules." These actions weaken the rule of law and pave the way for autocracy.

- Demagogues *"defer to prejudices, and ignorance, and even to popular jealousies and popular injustice, that a safe direction may be given to the publick [sic.] mind."* The ultimate aim of the demagogue is to apply the principles of democracy to every question—not just matters of public policy, but also questions of fact and questions of moral value. Everything is subject to a vote, and every proposed fact must be ratified by the *vox populi*. To flatter the people completely, the demagogue must pretend to accept their judgment on everything, and those who disagree with the public judgment (perhaps because they are experts in the field under discussion) must be castigated as both wrong and undemocratic. In this way, demagogues vanquish not just individual experts, but the entire concept of expertise: science, history, language, comparative politics, and all the rest of the things that people can spend their lives learning about vanish with a wave of the hand.

- *"This is a test that most often betrays the demagogue, for while loudest in proclaiming his devotion to the majority, he is, in truth, opposing the will of the entire people, in order to effect his purposes with a part.*" For all they may talk about the people as a coherent group, demagogues are actually devoted to pitting the people against each other. Demagogues rarely create new prejudices; they take the ones that already exist and amplify them, giving people permission to say things that had previously been unpopular or taboo. Much as demagogues work to weaken the rule of law, they try to weaken the social norms that enforce civic friendship, opening old wounds and encouraging the eruption of anger and hatred that have been kept below the surface by a thin, but crucially important layer of civility and civic decency.

This final point is especially important. Demagogues don't simply flatter the populace as a whole. They flatter a majority of the people by attacking and demonizing everyone else. Those who stand with the demagogue become "the people." Everybody else becomes effectively subhuman: "animals," "vermin," "criminals," "enemies of the state." In this way, demagogues ensure that a portion of the people will always side with them against their common enemy. At the same time, they create the perception of emergency to justify their destruction of the constitutional safeguards that would otherwise check their power. A demagogue needs division the way that a fire needs oxygen. They succeed only because they are able to fan the flames.

The only way to defeat a demagogue is to overcome the polarization that feeds their power. This is the advice of the Venezuelan economist and journalist Andrés Miguel Rondón, who was part of the opposition to the populist demagogue Hugo Chávez during his ten years in power. "Don't feed polarization, disarm it," Rondón wrote in *The Washington Post* reflecting on the mistakes that Chávez's opponents made:

It took opposition leaders 10 years to figure out that they needed to actually go to the slums and the countryside. Not for a speech or a rally, but for a game of dominoes or to dance salsa—to show they were Venezuelans, too, that they weren't just dour scolds and could hit a baseball, could tell a joke that landed. That they could break the tribal divide, come down off the billboards and show that they were real. This is not populism by other means. It is the only way of establishing your standing. It's deciding not to live in an echo chamber. To press pause on the siren song of polarization.

But demagogues need certain conditions to thrive, and they come with warning signs that we ignore at our peril. They require polarization, and they exploit it for their advantage, but they don't create it; it must be in place first, and it must have already weakened the norms and guardrails they intend to destroy. They tell us that people who don't look or think like we do are our enemies and that only they can protect us. They tell us that we are right and that nobody really understands us the way that they do. And they promise to hate who we hate and punish those who hate us. And if we believe them, they steal our democracy.

The demagogue is the ticking time bomb buried deep in democracy's basement; given enough time, they will always emerge and find a path to power. Democracies that survive find ways to expel their demagogues from power. Democracies that fail allow them to stay around long enough to destroy any mechanism that would allow the people to force them out. In 2016, the United States allowed a demagogue to come to power, and the cost to both our democracy and our standing in the world has already been severe. In November, we will have a chance to end the demagogue's career. It may well be the last chance we have.

This essay originally appeared on Medium *on June 18, 2020.*

BIDEN SHOULD MAKE TRUMP'S DEMAGOGUERY THE CAMPAIGN ISSUE OF ELECTION 2020

Eric Posner

With Joe Biden's lead in the polls, many Democrats and Republican Never-Trumpers are increasingly optimistic that President Donald Trump will lose in November.

But it would be a mistake to count Trump out. He has formidable advantages that will become more salient as the election nears. These advantages have nothing to do with his accomplishments or failures, and everything to do with his mastery of political theater.

For liberals, a dominant view is that, thanks to Trump's mishandling of the COVID-19 pandemic and the economic crisis it unleashed, Republican and Trump-leaning independent voters are coming to their senses.

But this is a sunny reading of events. Trump won the election in 2016 by converting his professional and temperamental unfitness for the presidency into a political virtue. Defiance of the establishment gave Trump credibility among Republican voters, who believed that mainstream politicians ignored their interests.

Trump solidified his support by stoking fears that immigrants were overrunning the country and threatening the dominance of white Americans. He offered himself as a savior. That was enough.

As illegal immigration has receded from the public imagination, Trump has sought new ways to capitalize on voters' fears.

He believes he has found it in the specter of urban criminality.

Trump clearly expects to benefit from the chaotic confrontations between police and protesters in America's big cities. No matter that most Americans sympathize with Black Lives Matter: if voters believe that crime and disorder will rise (as it has in places like Chicago) and that riots will erupt, their fears will take precedence over ideals of social justice.

Fearful people seek protection from powerful authority figures. No authority figure is more powerful than the sitting president of the United States, who oversees massive security resources. This is why so many observers worry that Trump's motive in sending federal paramilitary forces into U.S. cities was not to deter violence, but to provoke it.

As with illegal immigration, Trump has tried to tie peoples' fear for their safety with broader anxiety about cultural change. Just as Trump depicted illegal immigrants as criminals and threats to traditional American values, he portrays protesters as rioters and threats to American culture and history. They are not just lobbying Molotov cocktails; they are tearing down America's heroes.

The liberal media believes or hopes that Americans see through Trump's strategy, and blame the violence on him, not on the protesters. Maybe. But Trump is following in the footsteps of Richard Nixon, Ronald Reagan, and George H.W. Bush, all of whom provoked or exploited fears of urban crime and social decay on their way to the presidency.

Imagine it is October. Americans have forgotten about Trump's mishandling of the COVID-19 pandemic, which is subsiding as vaccines come to market or mask wearing and social distancing take hold and finally work. They are not terribly interested in Biden's promises to improve health care, address racial injustices, build infrastructure, or repair America's relationships with allies. They are worried about soaring crime rates, never-ending protests, and what they see as attacks from the left on traditional values and institutions. They trust Trump to tackle crime, and believe his warning that "Sleepy Joe" will disregard their fears.

In this scenario, Biden can choose among three responses. He could take the high road and point out that crime remains low by historical standards and is a local, not a federal, matter. He could argue that it is caused by childhood adversity that only well-designed federal social programs and police reforms can address. And he might also note that far more people in the U.S. have died as a result of Trump's bungled COVID-19 response than die from homicide in a typical year.

But, against a demagogue like Trump, the high road is a certain path to defeat. Fearful voters will not be satisfied by better statistical analysis or policy reforms that address the threat only indirectly.

The low road would involve a left or center-left style of demagoguery. Here, the goal is not to counter people's fear of crime but to redirect their fear to something else. Biden could try to stir up fear of the police, or of a police state helmed by Trump and manned by thuggish federal paramilitaries. Or he could follow the lead of classic populists from Huey Long to Hugo Chávez, and attack the rich and the corporate boogeyman as the source of all problems.

Biden can do neither. His decency works against him: an appeal to voters' primal fears will lack credibility. Nor would these tactics work. Few Americans want to defund the police— as Biden has already recognized. And Biden is too much a creature of the establishment to plausibly attack the rich.

Fortunately, Biden has a better strategy: to make Trump's demagoguery a theme of his campaign.

The last major American demagogue was Senator Joseph McCarthy, who held sway over U.S. politics from 1950 to 1954. McCarthy gained power by harping on the political establishment's alleged failure to oppose the Soviet threat and Communist influence.

McCarthy, like Trump, built on a real if thin empirical record. Communist efforts to subvert the U.S. government had been stopped by World War II's end. Drawing on public anxiety about Soviet expansionism, McCarthy inflated the threat with false accusations and manipulation of the press.

Yet McCarthy fell as quickly as he rose (he was censured by the Senate in 1954 and died in drunken obscurity in 1957). Perhaps Americans tired of his antics: none of his accusations led to a criminal conviction for espionage, undermining his credibility. Or perhaps he overreached by attacking the U.S. Army, which enjoyed more trust among Americans than did his earlier targets, which included the State Department and Hollywood.

The end came when McCarthy was called to account by Army lawyer Joseph Welch, who attacked the senator during a televised hearing for engaging in character assassination against one of Welch's colleagues. "Have you no sense of decency, sir? At long last, have you left no sense of decency?" he famously demanded of McCarthy, to the applause of spectators.

McCarthy's fate offers a glimmer of hope for Biden. Perhaps the American public can tolerate no more than four years of demagoguery. Many Trump voters do seem to have gotten the message that he has little to offer them except entertainment, and even that has been diminished by familiarity with Trump's shtick.

And Trump, like McCarthy, may have overreached when he challenged the army: by threatening to deploy military personnel to American cities, Trump breached a norm that separates the military from politics. If Trump again tries to embroil the army in domestic politics—he's backed off for now—Biden should call him to account for corrupting a respected institution.

But Biden's best strategy would be to draw voters' attention to the ways Trump has manipulated them.

Trump, like McCarthy, has exploited divisions between Americans, corrupted public debate with his lies and insults, and attacked valuable institutions, including the FBI and the Centers for Disease Control and Prevention, which Americans depend on. "Have you no sense of decency, Mr. Trump?" Biden should ask. The question answers itself.

This essay originally appeared in Project Syndicate *on August 10, 2020.*

WHAT BENJAMIN FRANKLIN WARNED US ABOUT

Joseph J. Ellis

A group of husky prisoners from the Philadelphia jail were carrying Benjamin Franklin on a stretcher back to his quarters after attending the last session of the Constitutional Convention in early September of 1787. The grandfather among the founding fathers was afflicted with a serious case of gout, but he had attended every session during that steamy hot summer. A well-dressed Philadelphia matron spied America's elder statesman and asked, "Mr. Franklin, what have you done?" "Given you a republic," Franklin replied, "if you can keep it."

Thus far, 233 years later, we have kept it. In fact, the United States is the oldest nation-sized republic in modern history. Between then and now, our republican framework has replaced the monarchical dynasties of Europe in the 19th century, then defeated the totalitarian despotisms of Germany, Japan, Italy and the Soviet Union in the 20th. What began as a bold experiment has become the global formula for national success in the western world.

There have been two occasions in American history when the fate of the republic was placed at risk. The first was the Civil War, when President Abraham Lincoln famously described the sectional conflict over slavery as "testing whether that nation or any nation so conceived and so dedicated can long endure?" The second was the Great Depression, which we survived under the leadership of FDR and his revised contract between democracy and capitalism called The New Deal.

We are currently on the cusp of a third serious challenge to our republican roots, which has emerged in the person of the first full-scale demagogue who was elected president. In truth, the founders would actually be surprised that it has taken this long to produce such a political creature. For they knew from their study of the Greek and Roman classics that republics were uniquely vulnerable to demagogues, because they were dependent on popular opinion, which was easily manipulated by fear-mongers brandishing conspiracy theories with potent appeal to the uneducated. During the founding era, Alexander Hamilton regarded Aaron Burr as just such a threat, and was challenged to a duel by Burr for making that accusation.

More recently, over the past four years, we have witnessed a demagogue challenge the republican principles in five areas of governance: Congress, led by the Republican Senate, has abdicated its constitutional obligation to check executive power; the Justice Department has shirked its responsibility to enforce the law fairly; misinformation and lies have become an acceptable norm for all members of the executive branch; a full generation of unqualified sycophants have been appointed to the federal judiciary; and the occupant of the White House has consistently maintained that he is above the law.

We can safely assume that Franklin is trembling in his grave, for these are all major deviations from republican principles. But they only become fatal changes if and when all these dictatorial improvisations seem institutionalized. And that can only occur if the current president is reelected in November, an election the results of which he refuses to say he will accept if it goes the other way. Then the American republic begins to die.

If, on the other hand, he departs as a one-term president, the damage he has inflicted, while considerable, is also repairable. In fact, we will be able to go forward with a clearer grasp of the reforms necessary to avert the election of future demagogues.

This is the chief reason why the looming election is the most important political event of our lifetime. This is not an election about personalities, the pandemic, the economy, or Black Lives Matter, though they are all on the ballot. This is an election to decide whether we wish to remain the American republic. Though the founders are busy being dead, their voices still linger in the atmosphere with a resoundingly clear answer to that question.

This essay originally appeared in CNN Opinion *on September 1, 2020.*

WHY AMERICA MUST NOT REELECT A DEMAGOGUE: THAT'S WHAT TRUMP IS, AND IT MATTERS

Eli Merritt

In addition to clinical diagnoses, such as narcissistic personality and delusional disorder, public commentators frequently dispense political diagnoses of President Trump. The most common are authoritarian, fascist, autocrat, dictator, totalitarian and demagogue. But only one of these, demagogue, is in fact accurate.

This distinction matters hugely at this juncture in our history, less than three weeks from a volatile presidential election, because if we have any hope of arresting our constitutional democracy's descent into chaos and breakdown, we must first know exactly what struck us in the fateful year 2016.

The terms fascist, authoritarian and the other labels often attached to Trump are incorrect because they do not apply to the early or middle stages of the deterioration of a constitutional democracy; they apply to the end stages. Today we are not at the end stage of our democracy. We are instead at an early crossroads where a full-blown demagogue has ascended to the White House.

Trump's election to the presidency has exposed the single greatest vulnerability—and most destructive force—present in a democracy. Aristotle breathlessly warned about it. So did Plato, Thucydides, Polybius, Livy, Edward Gibbon, Alexis de Tocqueville, the founders of the United States and Abraham Lincoln.

These statesmen and political philosophers uniformly

exhorted the guardians of democracy to beware demagogues. In their writings and speeches, they elaborate a golden rule of this free yet fragile form of government: that the citizens of a democracy must work together tirelessly, irrespective of political and party differences, to keep demagogues out of high office.

So concerned was Aristotle about this destabilizing political personality type that he employed the term "demagogue" 29 times in his treatise "Politics," sounding the alarm repeatedly on the baleful impact of "the intemperance of demagogues" on rational government.

In the Constitutional Convention of 1787, the founders referenced "demagogues" 21 times, frequently with respect to the dangers of a demagogue ascending to the presidency. George Mason of Virginia pronounced, rightly, that no worse evil can befall a democracy than "the mischievous influence of demagogues."

For the same reason, Abraham Lincoln advised Americans in an 1838 speech, entitled "The Perpetuation of our Political Institutions," to unite fiercely behind one inexorable survival strategy of constitutional democracies: the exclusion of demagogues from elected office. When such a person gains traction in politics, Lincoln counseled, "it will require the people to be united with each other, attached to the government and laws, and generally intelligent, to successfully frustrate his designs."

Demagogues injure democracies in two potent, long-lasting ways. First, they foster division and distrust among the people instead of unity of purpose. Demagogues do this in order to gain and retain power for personal benefit, not for the benefit of the people.

Second, and far more dangerous to a democracy, a demagogue is temperamentally wired to run roughshod over everything we hold dear in our representative government: the Constitution, Bill of Rights, impartial courts, the rule of law, institutional norms, truth-telling, and, not least, free and fair elections followed by the peaceful transfer of power.

A demagogue is compulsively driven to obtain power and popularity at all costs. There is no higher godhead or object outside the self to obey. As a result, sacred democratic institutions

become, for the demagogue, vexatious obstacles to be manipulated in the relentless quest for power and self-glory.

As Alexander Hamilton said in the Constitutional Convention,
demagogues "hate the controul of the Genl. Government."
Every democratic tradition and institution that stands in their
way, he and other political philosophers from across the ages
scream at us to understand, eventually gets neutralized.

As ancient and modern political scientists attest, a democracy cannot long survive the corroding influence particularly of
demagogues in the presidential chair. They break the faith, and
over time, magnificent constitutional democracies like ours
degenerate into all-out demagogic democracy. Then, in later
stages of decay, the people, exhausted by tumultuous demagogic government, finally submit to the stabilizing influence of
authoritarianism as the lesser of two evils.

The great paradox of democracy is that the people, who possess the power, sometimes vote demagogues into office who,
once there, tear apart the very system of government that elected them, stripping the people of their power.

The best way to protect against this insidious peril is through
the twin instruments of political courage in democracy's gatekeepers and the awesome power of voting.

Most immediately, we must get Trump's political diagnosis
right. He is a demagogue—and therefore a poison to democracy. Joe Biden is not. Voters must understand that clearly. The
health, and possibly survival, of our democracy depends upon
it.

This essay originally appeared in The New York Daily News *on
October 15, 2020.*

HIS DEMAGOGY

Jesse Wegman

This month, federal and state authorities arrested 13 Michigan men on terrorism, conspiracy and weapons charges. Six of the men are alleged to have been plotting to kidnap the state's governor, Gretchen Whitmer, with whom they were furious for imposing shutdowns, as most other governors did, in the early weeks of the pandemic.

Ms. Whitmer's actions most likely saved thousands of lives. The arrested men, along with hundreds of other anti-shutdown protesters who swarmed the State Capitol in Lansing, considered her a tyrant.

As the protests grew in April, President Trump could have supported a governor navigating a tough situation and reminded Americans about the importance of stopping the spread of the coronavirus. Instead, he tweeted, "LIBERATE MICHIGAN!"—a message that has to date received nearly 200,000 likes and almost 39,000 retweets. He tweeted the same of other states with Democratic governors and said the Second Amendment was "under siege." It was as though Mr. Trump saw himself as another anti-government insurgent.

The message seems to have come through loud and clear. Protesters became bolder, and some marched into the Michigan statehouse brandishing semiautomatic rifles and long guns, forcing a shutdown of the State Legislature. Many political leaders rightly condemned the armed display. Mr. Trump defended the protesters. "These are very good people, but they are angry," he wrote on Twitter.

As Ms. Whitmer said after this month's arrests: "Hate groups heard the president's words not as a rebuke, but as a rallying cry. As a call to action. When our leaders speak, their words matter. They carry weight. When our leaders meet with, encourage or fraternize with domestic terrorists, they legitimize their actions, and they are complicit. When they stoke and contribute to hate speech, they are complicit."

Even after the arrests and charges, Mr. Trump has refused to rebuke violent agitators. Instead, he keeps feeding the fire. Speaking on Fox Business on Thursday, he said of Ms. Whitmer: "She wants to be a dictator in Michigan. And the people can't stand her."

A president's words are among his most powerful, and potentially dangerous, tools. They can rally the American public to work together toward a common cause. They can soothe the jangled nerves of a frightened nation, or provide a healing balm at a time of mourning. They can move global financial markets, start wars—and embolden violent individuals.

From the start of his campaign for president in 2015, Mr. Trump has gleefully upturned every expectation Americans had about how their presidents speak. He revels in crude insults, trivial gripes and constant mockery of those who disagree with him.

This is harmful on many levels. "The president isn't just the chief of the executive branch, but the head of state," said Ian Bassin, who worked in the White House Counsel's Office during the Obama administration and now runs the nonprofit group Protect Democracy. "That means part of what the presidency is about is norm-setting. When a president establishes that it's OK to make fun of people with disabilities, or to be racist, or to lie, or to assault women, you see that replicated in society. That's not a surprise."

Mr. Trump doesn't just mock his enemies. He demonizes and dehumanizes them. His attacks have resulted in his targets—whether a lawmaker like Representative Ilhan Omar of Minnesota, a television personality like the former Fox News anchor Megyn Kelly, a government scientist like Dr. Anthony Fauci, or a regular American citizen—getting swamped with death threats, and in some cases requiring personal protection.

The violent rhetoric, and its consequences, began almost as soon as Mr. Trump's campaign for the White House did.

In August 2015, barely two months after Mr. Trump announced his presidential bid by accusing Mexican immigrants of being "rapists," two Boston men beat a homeless man with a metal pipe and then urinated on him. "Donald Trump was right," one of the men said, according to the police. "All these illegals need to be deported."

Mr. Trump tweeted out a condemnation of the attack, calling it "terrible" and saying, "I would never condone violence." But repeatedly on the campaign trail, he did just that.

At a February 2016 campaign rally, he told his supporters: "If you see somebody getting ready to throw a tomato, knock the crap out of them, would you? Seriously. Just knock the hell out of them. I promise you, I will pay for the legal fees."

A few weeks later he said of one protester, "I'd like to punch him in the face, I'll tell you."

At another rally, a protester being escorted out by the police was sucker-punched. Mr. Trump called the attack "very, very appropriate" and the kind of action "we need a little bit more of."

In August 2016, he warned that if Hillary Clinton was elected, she would appoint Supreme Court justices who would rule in favor of gun control laws. "Nothing you can do, folks," Mr. Trump said, before adding, "Although the Second Amendment people—maybe there is, I don't know."

This language was dangerous enough coming from a candidate. With Mr. Trump's ascension to the most powerful job in the country, the stakes got only higher, and his reach broader.

A few months after his inauguration, he told a gathering of police officers that they should rough up the people they arrest. "Please don't be too nice," Mr. Trump said, to laughter and cheers.

When a Republican representative from Montana physically assaulted a reporter who had asked a question, Mr. Trump praised the lawmaker. "Any guy that can do a body-slam," Mr. Trump said, "he's my guy."

In May, Mr. Trump responded to protests against police brutality by saying, "When the looting starts, the shooting starts." When the shooting did start, he defended one person accused of gunfire: a 17-year-old boy who drove 20 miles to a Wisconsin protest armed with a semiautomatic rifle, which he allegedly used to shoot three people, killing two of them. It was self-defense, Mr. Trump suggested days after the teenager was charged with murder.

At the presidential debate last month, Mr. Trump was asked to condemn white supremacists without equivocation. He would not. Instead, he instructed the violent right-wing group the Proud Boys to "stand back and stand by."

Mr. Trump and his defenders regularly claim that he is being misunderstood and say that he has condemned violence and white supremacy more than any president in history. The president is asked to condemn violence so often because violence is so often committed in his name. The Proud Boys, for one, did not take his words as a condemnation. "I think he was saying I appreciate you and appreciate your support," the group's founder said after the debate.

Trump supporters are not the only people who commit acts of political violence. But Mr. Trump has been invoked in dozens of acts of violence, threats of violence or allegations of assault, according to a review of five years of criminal cases by ABC News.

The victims of some of the worst attacks have been from the minority groups that Mr. Trump so often targets with his words. In addition to the 2015 attack on the homeless man in Boston, there was the terror campaign involving more than a dozen pipe bombs sent to prominent journalists and critics of Mr. Trump by a Trump supporter. There was the massacre in an El Paso Walmart that left 23 dead; minutes before the attack, the 21-year-old suspect said he was doing it as a response to "the Hispanic invasion of Texas." And there was the slaughter of 51 people during prayer in two New Zealand mosques by a right-wing zealot who said he saw Mr. Trump as "a symbol of renewed white identity and common purpose."

In 2017, a federal judge in Kentucky ruled that Mr. Trump could be sued by protesters who had been assaulted at a 2016 rally where he had said, "Get 'em out of here!" That statement was "an order, an instruction, a command," the judge said, and the protesters' injuries were "a direct and proximate result" of Mr. Trump's words. The case was dismissed on appeal, but the judge was right: Mr. Trump's supporters know that his first response is the truest expression of his beliefs, and

Mr. Trump, for all his dissembling, knows exactly what he is saying.

This harm won't end with Mr. Trump's presidency. His toxic rhetoric has filtered down to elementary and secondary schools around the country, where children have been repeating the president's most vile language for the past five years. In hundreds of cases, children have reported being mocked, harassed or attacked for being Hispanic, Black or Muslim, according to a survey by *The Washington Post*. Many of the incidents have made reference to Mr. Trump's border wall, including one case last year in which a 13-year-old New Jersey boy told a Mexican-American classmate that "all Mexicans should go back behind the wall." Soon after, the 13-year-old assaulted the boy and knocked his mother unconscious.

"It's gotten way worse since Trump got elected," said Ashanty Bonilla, a Mexican-American high school student who endured so much ridicule from classmates that she changed schools. "They hear it. They think it's OK. The president says it. ... Why can't they?"

This essay originally appeared in The New York Times *on October 16, 2020.*

III. JANUARY 6 ATTACK ON THE U.S. CAPITOL

MY FELLOW REPUBLICANS, TRUMP IS DESTROYING US

Jeff Flake

Today, in what is meant to be a solemn ritual of democracy, Congress meets in joint session to consecrate the will of the American people and mark the election of Joe Biden as president.

Unfortunately, President Trump refuses to accept the reality of his substantial loss, and so becomes determined to create an alternate reality in which he won. As he crosses that rubicon, Mr. Trump has taken many in my party with him, all of whom seem to have learned the wrong lessons from this anomalous presidency. George Orwell, after all, meant for his work to serve as a warning, not as a template.

How many injuries to American democracy can my Republican Party tolerate, excuse and champion? It is elementary to have to say so, but for democracy to work one side must be prepared to accept defeat. If the only acceptable outcome is for your side to win, and a loser simply refuses to lose, then America is imperiled.

I once had a career in public life—six terms in the House of Representatives and another six years in the Senate—and then the rise of a dangerous demagogue, and my party's embrace of him, ended that career. Or rather, I chose not to go along with my party's rejection of its core conservative principles in favor of that demagogue. In a speech on the Senate floor on Oct. 24, 2017, I announced that because of the turn my party had taken, I would not run for re-election: the career of a politician that is complicit in undermining his own values doesn't mean much.

As a lifelong conservative Republican, I was surprised to find myself so profoundly at odds with my own party and with the man who had used its ballot line to vault to power. But the values that made me a conservative and an American were indeed being undermined, the country was paying a steep price for it, and I would be a liar to my family, my state and my conscience if I were to pretend otherwise.

It is hard to comprehend how so many of my fellow Republicans were able—and are still able—to engage in the fantasy that they had not abruptly abandoned the principles they claimed to believe in. It is also difficult to understand how this betrayal could be driven by deference to the unprincipled, incoherent and blatantly self-interested politics of Donald Trump, defined as it is by its chaos and boundless dishonesty. The conclusion that I have come to is that they did it for the basest of reasons—sheer survival and rank opportunism.

But survival divorced from principle makes a politician unable to defend the institutions of American liberty when they come under threat by enemies foreign and domestic. And keeping your head down in capitulation to a rogue president makes you little more than furniture. One wonders if that is what my fellow Republicans had in mind when they first sought public office.

But if it was my obligation to end my congressional career by speaking out in defiance, then my time in Congress had begun in awe.

It was the first few days of my first term in Congress— Saturday, Jan. 6, 2001, 20 years ago today—when I witnessed an act of civic faith that was simply extraordinary. With utmost fidelity to our founding principles and the reverence the United States Constitution deserves, one presidential administration handed over power to another, peacefully and with dignity, after the most highly contentious election in more than a century, an election decided by just a few hundred votes in a single state. Perhaps most moving of all was that this ritual transition of our democracy had over the time since our founding become so ordinary.

A kid from Snowflake, Ariz., doesn't often get to witness such history, and so I kept a journal:

The family flew home on Friday afternoon. I had to stay until Saturday afternoon because the House and Senate met in joint session to count electoral votes. Given the disputed election, there were fears that the Democrats would try to pull something. A dozen or so House Democrats did object to the Florida electoral votes, but because they failed to get any Senate Democrats to sign on with them, they failed to thwart the proceedings. It was quite a spectacle nonetheless. Vice President Al Gore, who presided over this historic meeting, was forced to call the game for his opponent, George W. Bush. I met Gore afterward, who had to be feeling pretty rotten to have won the popular vote but to have lost in the Electoral College.

One thing I left out of my journal entry was that in affirming that his opponent, George W. Bush, would be our next president, Mr. Gore said this: "May God bless our new president and new vice president, and may God bless the United States of America."

Mr. Gore's was an act of grace that the American people had every right to expect of someone in his position, a testament to the robustness and durability of American constitutional democracy. That he was merely doing his job and discharging his responsibility to the Constitution is what made the moment both profound and ordinary.

Vice President Mike Pence must do the same today. As we are now learning, a healthy democracy is wholly dependent on the good will and good faith of those who offer to serve it.

Today, the American people deserve to witness the majesty of a peaceful transfer of power, just as I saw, awe-struck, two decades ago. Instead, we find ourselves in this bizarre condition of our own making, two weeks from the inauguration of a new president, with madness unspooling from the White House, grievous damage to our body politic compounding daily.

My fellow Republicans, as Secretary of State Brad Raffensperger of Georgia has shown us this week, there is power in standing up to the rank corruptions of a demagogue. Mr. Trump can't hurt you. But he is destroying us.

This essay originally appeared in The New York Times *on January 6, 2021.*

HOW TO PROTECT AMERICA FROM THE NEXT DONALD TRUMP

Bryan Garsten

Voting Donald Trump out of office was crucial, but it will not be enough to save the American experiment.

Many critics have used the words "authoritarian" or "fascist" to describe the president's mode of politics, as if he were an invader from outside our democratic way of life. In fact, Mr. Trump is a creature native to our own style of government and therefore much more difficult to protect ourselves against: He is a demagogue, a popular leader who feeds on the hatred of elites that grows naturally in democratic soil. We have almost forgotten how common such creatures are in democracies because we have relied on a technology designed to restrain them: the Constitution. It has worked by setting up rules for us to follow, but also on a deeper level by shaping our sense of what we are proud of and what we are ashamed of in our common life. Today this constitutional culture has all but collapsed, and with it, our protection against demagogues.

For most of the history of Western political thought, writers focused on demagogy only in the context of arguing that democracy was a poor form of government. Aristocratic critics such as Thucydides and Plato blamed popular leaders for dismissing experts, exploiting the poor and soaking the rich, sparking factional violence, and starting foreign wars to distract the populace from their tyrannical tendencies. Since these writers thought it obvious that democracies were natural breeding grounds for demagogues, their strategy for eliminating demagogy was to support alternatives to democratic government: If you don't like wolves, don't create a wolf habitat.

The framers of our Constitution were not satisfied with that anti-democratic view, but they were persuaded that a democracy would not work well unless it found ways to defang demagogues. They thought of their constitution-making as an experiment to see whether they could "refine and enlarge" the democratic will, in Madison's words, civilizing the inevitable conflict between popular leaders and elites and channeling it into a sustainable form of politics. Right now, the experiment is not succeeding.

The language Mr. Trump uses, his willingness to insult, his refusal to follow the standard conventions of polite society or decency—his crudeness—is not a superficial sideshow. It is his defining trait, both a rebuke of Madison's experiment and a giveaway that he is a demagogue.

Look for the common thread in his otherwise unconnected actions: Associating ordinary immigrants with rapists and murderers was not necessary to demonstrate a commitment to lowering crime or saving American jobs; it was a way of showing he would say what others would not. Tearing a mask off on the White House balcony did not help the economy; it was a declaration of independence from the rule of experts. Trolling the media on whether to accept the results of the election; refusing to offer, on a journalist's command, the requisite statement opposing white nationalists; and declining to apologize as if backing down would compromise his principles—these are positions whose substance should not be ignored, and I find them morally appalling—but we understand the fundamental political dynamic better when we focus less on their content and more on their motivation: He is determined to show that he will not be *shamed*.

To allow oneself to be shamed is to admit that you are subject to and ruled by society's arbiters of what is acceptable. Demagogues, as a rule, insist that they will not be so ruled; that is part of their democratic appeal. Shame is a constraint, and so is an affront to freedom. Shame condemns from a moral high ground, and so is an affront to equality. The demagogue follows these impoverished understandings of freedom and equality and concludes that conventions and laws are for suckers. Part of his pernicious influence is to persuade even his opponents that moral and constitutional scruples are forms of weakness.

The demagogue's own weakness lies in the fact that most people, even most of his supporters, tend to live by the conventions that he disdains. He needs their support and craves their adoration, making him dependent on people he holds in contempt—in this case, on evangelicals and suburban women. In both his shamelessness and the political dilemma it creates for him we can see how well this president fits into the classic demagogic type.

Historians and political theorists differ about how and when we abandoned the constitutional culture condemning demagogy. Some blame Newt Gingrich's strategic decision to have congressional candidates campaign against the very institution they aimed to join, while others point to the McGovern-Fraser Commission's democratization of party primaries after the 1968 Democratic convention. Some claim that well-meaning efforts at governmental transparency have allowed lobbyists, campaigns and advertising-hungry media to ruin the prospect of real deliberation in congressional committees, while others look further back, blaming Woodrow Wilson for arguing that the Constitution had to evolve to allow stronger presidential leadership. Or did the societal disgust for demagogy last through all of that, only to be finally dissolved by our rush into the pandering algorithms of social media and the tribalism of Twitter?

Whichever story we tell about the past, the work in front of us remains. We could start by repairing the parts of the constitutional structure that were supposed to insulate our leaders from the temptation to be demagogues and give them incentives to take responsibility for long-term results. The constitutional framers hoped that distributing power among the states, channeling political ambition toward offices with clearly circumscribed but overlapping powers, keeping the Senate small and senators' terms long, and filtering presidential elections through state legislatures would all help contain demagogues.

It is a stain on our country's honor that these anti-demagogic parts of our constitution were sullied by their use to defend slavery and Jim Crow. In acknowledging that historical fact, however, we can't let ourselves off the hook for dealing with the general problem they were meant to address. Any serious constitutional reform would consider not only which party benefits from these institutions, but also how best to balance responsiveness and responsibility. Political parties and the media regulatory environment need reform too—but in devising strategies we should be thinking not only about openness but also about how to create the conditions in which we, the people, are most likely to resist demagogic appeals and make our own best judgments.

The college-educated elite and well-meaning technocrats may say that expert rule is the only alternative to demagogues, but they are wrong. When we allow them to rule, we fuel popular frustration and drive people into the arms of demagogues in reaction. The real alternative is to strengthen our ability to govern ourselves well by supporting the kinds of schools and jobs that train us in the habits of citizenship, by creating the background conditions in which we can solve more problems in our families and communities, and by reforming electoral systems and legislative procedures to strengthen the incentives for politicians to move beyond demagogy. Too many of us are guilty of prioritizing immediate policy outcomes over the work of maintaining a system of self-government that will bring out the best in us over the long term.

These sorts of reforms will only work, however, if they help us find our way out of a demagogic society and into a constitutional culture in which leaders feel ashamed for not helping us "refine and enlarge" our political passions. Plato wrote that demagogues were like the makers of pastries who give us what we crave in the moment but not what will make us healthy. Do we now allow the modern equivalent of pastry chefs to dominate our society? Literally, yes: We subsidize corn syrup and pay the price in health care. Figuratively, yes: We refuse to regulate social media even as it titrates dopamine in a way designed to distract us from serious projects into one click after another. Economically, yes: We rely on ever-growing consumer demand, confusing freedom with the ability to increase the size and intensity of our desires in a way that ensures we are never satisfied. We cultivate in ourselves impatience, impertinence and insatiability—the very qualities of a demagogue.

Allowing our desires to grow always larger is like spending our lives trying to fill a sieve, or welcoming a lifetime of itchiness so that we can always have the satisfaction of scratching ourselves again. These are Plato's analogies from thousands of years ago, meant to make us feel ashamed for not aiming at something higher.

Once the election is over, shame may be a more constructive emotion than anger. Anger will continue to set us against one another in cycles of blame and vengeance, but shame could bring us together into an effort at self-correction. If the intensified demagogy we have seen lately comes about partly from our own mismanagement of our constitutional democracy, then a solution will require a hard look in the mirror. The demagogues themselves will not do this, but demagogues can be managed through their dependence on us. Will we become ashamed at having allowed ourselves to be so caught up in scratching our own itches that we let a critical mass of our fellow citizens think a vulgar charlatan was their last, best hope? Could it be that we've had the leader we deserved? We should aim to deserve better. The first step toward self-government is to recognize that the challenges do not all, or even mainly, come from fascistic authoritarians foreign to democracy but from ourselves and our way of life.

This essay originally appeared in The New York Times *on November 9, 2020.*

TRUMP PROVIDED A ROAD MAP FOR STEALING AN ELECTION. NEXT TIME COULD BE WORSE

Curtis A. Bradley

The phenomenon of Donald Trump shook many people out of the complacent belief that our democracy was functioning smoothly. But once Trump is out of office, there is a danger that a narrative will emerge celebrating how well the guardrails of our system ultimately performed—despite Trump's demagoguery. Already, hints of this story are evident: "The U.S. Election System Worked," argued two scholars in an article published just two days after Election Day. In *The Economist*, Harvard Law School's Jack Goldsmith observed—in an otherwise sobering account—that "the most remarkable fact about [Trump's] presidency is how well the American constitutional system stood up to and survived it."

Despite Trump's disrespect for the rule of law, the narrative might go, the courts functioned, the press remained free, and—knock on wood—we'll see a peaceful transition of power. Democracy will have defeated Trump's authoritarian impulses.

One problem with this story is that Trump revealed how many of the guardrails of our democracy are built on norms rather than on law, and he made clear the limits of the constraining effect of norms. These norms include a basic level of honesty by public officials (so that voters can make informed decisions) and a respect for democratic outcomes by those who lose elections. In ignoring these and other baseline assumptions of the U.S. political system, Trump has not only sown doubt and division in the country but also opened the way for others to do the same.

Trump was a serial liar throughout his presidency, and he and his allies launched an especially vigorous disinformation campaign in the wake of the election, claiming without evidence that there had been massive voter fraud and that the election had been "stolen" from him. Even though courts and election officials—Republican and Democratic—have consistently rejected these claims, millions of Americans believe them.

In an earlier period of our history, traditional news sources might have served as an important guardrail against a flagrantly dishonest president—as they did, for example, during Watergate. But Trump undercut this check throughout his presidency by constantly labeling unfavorable information as "fake news" and by relying on conservative media outlets to offer voters an alternate reality more favorable to him.

Trump's ability to distort the truth has been abetted by the rise of social media and the general disaggregation of information outlets, diminishing the influence of traditional news sources. Indeed, even though the media highlighted and documented countless acts of dishonesty and abuse of power by Trump throughout his presidency, he still managed to receive more than 73 million votes.

In years past, one might also have expected members of Congress—especially moderate members of the president's party—to check a president's excesses. But moderate members of Congress are a dying breed, and extreme partisanship is the new reality. Republican legislators in general have lived in constant fear that Trump would direct his wrath and retribution at them should they publicly question his conduct—and that they would pay a price at the polls. Faced with the possibility of losing party support, many chose silence.

Trump's presidency has revealed the limitations of other institutional guardrails, as well. Many people had high hopes that Robert S. Mueller III, acting as special counsel, would get to the bottom of Russia's efforts to interfere with the 2016 election and the Trump campaign's potential connections to those efforts. But Mueller was hampered by constraints on his team's ability to gather information, due to, among other things, Trump's refusal to be interviewed. And because of existing Department of Justice policy, Mueller also felt bound not to consider whether the president was guilty of a crime. While Mueller's report nevertheless contained damaging information, including about obstruction of justice, this information was misrepresented by Trump's attorney general before it was released to the public and distorted by Trump and his allies in Congress.

Impeachment is the ultimate constitutional tool for dealing with a corrupt executive. The Democratic-controlled House tried to apply this guardrail after it emerged that Trump had tried to coerce a foreign leader to develop fake dirt on Trump's chief political opponent, a gross abuse of power. The House indeed impeached him, but partisanship again prevailed in the Senate—a body that, in 2020, seems a far cry from what Alexander Hamilton described in Federalist No. 65 as a tribunal that would have the "necessary impartiality" to pass judgment on a president's conduct. Trump not only weathered the impeachment storm but became politically stronger as a result. Impeachment does not seem like much of a limitation on the executive in today's politically polarized environment.

It has been clear for some time that another test for the system would be whether Trump would accept the election results if he lost. Even now, weeks after the election, the answer is no. Another test was whether Republicans would pressure him to concede defeat; again the answer is no, or at least not very much. Indeed, initially a number of key Republicans in Congress affirmatively supported Trump's baseless claims of election fraud. Many Republicans have finally begun to accept the reality of Trump's election loss, but only after weeks of waiting while Trump probed for ways to overturn the result.

Trump's attempt to reverse the election's outcome through lawsuits, a blizzard of conspiracy theories, and the recruitment of allies in state legislatures has not succeeded, but not because the system is incorruptible. Trump's litigation team was especially inept, but a future Trump may have more skilled representation. Trump also faced an almost impossible task of reversing the outcomes in several states, but imagine if the election had been a bit closer and it had come down to just one or two states, or if there had been more plausible disputes about the accuracy of the vote counts. Faced with pressure by Trump's allies, some state officials like Georgia Secretary of State Brad Raffensperger (a Republican) held firm in defending the counts, but—as the behavior of many Senate Republicans makes clear—such courage and character are not guaranteed, especially given the death threats and career consequences that principled Republican state officials are experiencing now.

A decisive number of state officials in Michigan and elsewhere declined to take Trump up on his invitation to block or delay certification of the election results, and they have resisted his suggestion that they seat alternative electors. But there is nothing in our system that completely rules out such end runs around the democratic process. A few key individuals respected the norms that make our democracy work—this time. But other officials might make a different choice next time, particularly if they are installed in order to make a different choice next time.

The lesson from all of this cannot possibly be how effectively the guardrails of democracy have performed. The lesson, rather, is how narrowly our nation escaped disaster. We have been fortunate that Trump's malevolence and corruption have been tempered by his incompetence, but we should not let the preservation of our democracy rest on luck. We must strengthen the guardrails of our democracy before a more skilled demagogue comes along and steals a presidential election with the help of enough strategically positioned state officials to do his bidding.

This essay originally appeared in The Washington Post *on November 30, 2020.*

DONALD TRUMP UNLEASHED HIS CULT ON AMERICAN DEMOCRACY

James Risen

I t happened here. Donald Trump unleashed his cult on American democracy on Wednesday.

QAnon conspiracy theorists, far-right Proud Boys, and other white nationalist Trump cultists stormed and ransacked the U.S. Capitol. After order was eventually restored, fellow members of Trump's cult—a handful of senators and more than a hundred members of the House of Representatives— voted to try to overturn the presidential election in a bid to keep Trump in power. Both efforts failed, but the riot in the Capitol building and the coup-by-legislative-fiat later that night were part of the same autocratic impulse: a deep yearning for a strongman. Sens. Josh Hawley and Ted Cruz, the leaders of the coup attempt in the Senate, might as well have been personally leading the Trump cultists as they rampaged through the Capitol's corridors.

There are no political subtleties, no nuanced hot takes about what happened in Washington on January 6, 2021. It was an insurrection, period. It was an insurrection by a Trump mob, and later by their confederates in the House and Senate.

January 6, 2021, had clear echoes of February 27, 1933: the day of the Reichstag fire in Berlin, when the Nazis torched Germany's legislative building, four weeks after Adolf Hitler had been sworn in as the German chancellor. The fire provided a pretext for Hitler to assume emergency powers and become the country's dictator, while the Nazis framed a leftist immigrant for the arson, claiming it was all a Communist plot—just as right-wing Republicans are now falsely claiming that the pro-Trump rioters in the Capitol on Wednesday were actually "antifa" members in disguise. And it is no accident that there were reportedly a number of neo-Nazi sympathizers in the pro-Trump mob at the U.S. Capitol.

January 6, 2021, also had echoes of July 12, 1864. The Confederacy—the Southern slavocracy that is the precursor to today's pro-Trump white nationalist movement—came closest to occupying Washington on that date; Confederate Gen. Jubal Early marched his troops on the capital, only to be stopped by Union troops at Fort Stevens near the border between Washington, D.C., and Maryland. President Abraham Lincoln was in Fort Stevens at the time, and legend has it that Oliver Wendell Holmes, then a Union officer and a future Supreme Court justice, had to tell the president to keep his head down.

It is no accident that one of the most widely seen photographs from Wednesday's rampage inside the Capitol showed a Trump cultist marching down a corridor carrying a large Confederate flag.

In 1935, Sinclair Lewis wrote a political novel that was a thinly veiled warning about demagogue Huey Long. The novel's title, *It Can't Happen Here*, has become a comforting line for American political observers ever since: that the United States is too deeply rooted in the rule of law and a constitutional system of government for a dictatorship to rise up.

Trump may have failed to break the American system this time, but he has provided a road map for future demagogues. Unfortunately, he has revealed that it is not as difficult as once thought. Many of the constraints on autocracy that Americans thought were built into the constitutional system were actually just norms, traditions and guidelines, and Trump has proven how easily they could be swept away.

This dangerous ending has been coming ever since Trump rode down the elevator at Trump Tower on June 16, 2015, and announced his presidential campaign. Everything Trump has done as president was there to be seen—openly and obviously—from the day he announced his candidacy, through his upset win in the 2016 presidential election. The lies, conspiracy theories, racism, corruption, and criminality—Trump never hid any of it.

And yet far too many chose to ignore the danger.

Trump's enablers have been legion. There is Mark Burnett, the television producer who helped Trump create his false public persona on *The Apprentice*. There is Jeff Zucker, the NBC Universal chief who signed Trump to the show and later, as head of CNN during the 2016 presidential campaign, allowed candidate Trump to foment his demagoguery on endless loops on CNN in a bid for higher ratings.

There is Rupert Murdoch and his family, who turned Fox News into Trump's propaganda and disinformation arm, poisoning the minds of millions of Trump followers.

There is Jack Dorsey, founder of Twitter, who allowed Trump to turn his Twitter account into a deadly political weapon. The enormous attention Trump brought to Dorsey's platform helped aggrandize his company.

There were the billionaire fundraisers who backed Trump, from Blackstone CEO Stephen Schwarzman to Sheldon Adelson, eager for tax cuts or more extreme pro-Israel policies.

And there were the Republican politicians who were initially repulsed by Trump and then became his slavish followers, when they realized their political careers depended on tapping into Trump's demagogic fury.

All of these enablers had one thing in common: They didn't take Trump seriously enough. Now, in Trump's final days in office, many of them have finally been shaken by what they helped unleash.

The Murdoch family finally broke with Trump when Fox News actually called the 2020 election accurately, infuriating Trump when it was among the first news organizations to call the critical state of Arizona for Biden. In response, many of Trump's cultish followers have been turning to new Trump propaganda outlets. As for Dorsey, Twitter temporarily suspended Trump's account in the wake of the mob violence Wednesday, while warning of a permanent suspension. Schwartzman finally broke with Trump as well, issuing a statement saying that he was "shocked and horrified" by the mob's actions.

Senate Majority Leader Mitch McConnell also finally stood up to Trump on Wednesday, denouncing the efforts to steal the presidential election. "The voters, the courts, and the states have all spoken," McConnell said, before the Capitol was breached. "If we overrule them all, it would damage our republic forever."

Senator Lindsey Graham finally stood up to Trump Wednesday night as well, saying "Trump and I have had a hell of a journey, but enough is enough."

Like Schwartzman and McConnell, Graham had stood by Trump through four years of carnage. Only when Graham and other senators were forced to seek shelter from the mob they helped unleash did Graham finally break with Trump.

By Thursday, a few Trump administration officials had resigned after Trump's incitement of Wednesday's riot, including Education Secretary Betsy DeVos and Transportation Secretary Elaine Chao, who is McConnell's wife.

Some administration officials and congressional leaders were also considering whether to try to remove Trump from office early so he can't commit any more unconstitutional and criminal acts before President-elect Joe Biden's inauguration on January 20. House Speaker Nancy Pelosi and Senator Charles Schumer, who is about to become Senate majority leader thanks to the Democratic sweep of both Senate seats in Georgia this week, called for Trump's removal from office on Thursday, and even a Republican member of Congress, Representative Adam Kinzinger of Illinois, called for Trump's removal through the invocation of the 25th Amendment. Pelosi is also canvassing House Democrats about impeaching Trump again.

What is most frightening is that anonymous members of Trump's own administration have suggested to reporters that they fear Trump is now mentally unbalanced. Following the riot at the Capitol, *The Washington Post* reported that one administration official described Trump as being "a total monster" on Wednesday.

January 20 can't get here soon enough.

This essay originally appeared in The Intercept *on January 8, 2021.*

STORMING OF THE CAPITOL FUELED BY DEMAGOGUERY AND THREAT TO REPUBLICAN DEMOCRACY

Yaël Ossowski

L ast Wednesday, we saw the worst passions of the American republic storm through the doors of the U.S. Capitol in Washington.

For hours, people around the world watched as protestors transformed into rioters who ransacked various congressional offices, posed for photos on the House floor, and terrorized hundreds of congressmen and women, senators, staff, journalists, and Capitol Police.

One woman, a protestor and rioter from Arizona, was shot and killed by Capitol Police. Three others died due to medical emergencies, according to Washington Police Chief Robert Contee.

The march outflowed from a "Stop the Steal" rally held by President Donald Trump in the hours prior, decrying the results of the 2020 election and fueling various allegations of voter fraud and manipulation.

He urged his supporters at the rally to turn their attention to Congress, which was deliberating the final tally of the Electoral College votes.

What transpired at the Capitol Wednesday was something no one should tolerate in a liberal democracy. The ransacking of a seat of the federal government, by any force or group of individuals, is an act of aggression that should be prosecuted.

It was, no doubt, a result of demagoguery and a violent urging by Donald Trump.

There are many items of concern that my organization and I have broadly agreed with President Trump: on questioning the role of the World Health Organization early on in the pandemic, dismantling burdensome regulations that quash innovation, pushing for the safe and orderly opening of the economy after devastating coronavirus restrictions, and more.

At the same time, we have opposed the Trump administration when it was needed most: disastrous tariffs that raise prices for all consumers, drug pricing plans that will set back innovation while making drugs more expensive, and a federal vaping flavor ban that will deprive former smokers of the ability to choose a less harmful alternative.

Personally, I have opposed Trump's desire to severely restrict and reduce immigration. My family immigrated to the U.S. some 30 years ago, and we have enjoyed a much more fruitful life because of it.

But those policy arguments and disagreements are secondary to the very real threat of a violent parade of hysteria through the halls of the Capitol.

We advocate for ideas to improve society based on the rule of law and democratic order. We use the means of free expression, free assembly, and the right to petition our government to ensure that policies that help every consumer and every citizen will be the law of the land.

Seeing a mob trample into the primary seat of one of America's branches of government achieves none of that, and should be rightly condemned.

Our decentralized republican democracy based on a time-honored Constitution, a system that is unique to the United States and has allowed for some of the most promising economic and social innovation in the world, was threatened. And we cannot excuse these actions in the slightest.

From this point forward, we must restore the rule of law and advocate for liberal democratic principles to advance the American project.

That President Trump should continue to serve out the last two weeks of his term, after this insurrection and rebellion in our nation's capital, is unacceptable.

Whether it be through his removal from office by the invocation of the 25th Amendment by Vice President Mike Pence and the cabinet, or articles of impeachment in the House and swift conviction by the Senate, something must be done to show to the world what happens when order and liberty are transgressed in a representative liberal democracy.

When the actions of certain individuals go too far, and when demagoguery threatens the very system that allows us to freely enjoy our liberty and pursue happiness how we see fit, that is an appropriate time to use the tools at our disposal to rectify injustice.

Let us hope justice conquers after the events of this week.

This essay originally appeared in Inside Sources *on January 10, 2021.*

HOW TO BREAK
THE DEMAGOGUE CYCLE

Michael Signer

L
ater this month, the Senate will come back into session and will soon consider whether to convict Donald Trump, following his bipartisan impeachment by the House of Representatives. The Senate must vote to convict Trump, even though by then he will be out of office and a private citizen. The reason is that only by convicting Trump can the Senate proceed to an even more important vote: to disqualify him from ever holding public office again. And this is absolutely necessary for preserving American democracy in faith with the history, and the principles, that undergird the United States Constitution.

Disqualification may seem, at first glance, like simple retribution or partisan posturing. It is anything but. Disqualification is in fact the fulcrum on which the Constitution's democratic institutions, and its underlying theory, turn. Its roots run to the ancient observations about democracy's core fragility that guided the framers in their design of the Constitution. In this president's case, disqualification is imperative, fulfilling the Constitution's essential purpose of defending democracy from the most lethal foe: a homegrown demagogue like Trump.

Ancient philosophers and statesmen saw such demagogues as keys to a devastating "cycle of regimes." The Greek historian Polybius observed that a demagogue who was "sufficiently ambitious and daring" could capture the people's favor, where they "once more found a master and a despot." What followed the demagogue's "reign of mere violence"? "Tumultuous assemblies, massacres, banishments."

Ancient Athens had tried to break this cycle. After suffering through ruinous wars and rampant corruption brought on by a spate of demagogues, Athens passed a law allowing citizens to vote, using small pieces of pottery on which they scratched names, to ostracize—to exile for 10 years—any politician "violating democratic principles." As *The Economist* recently noted, Athenian ostracism was equivalent to impeachment and was "at the heart of the Athenian political system."

The framers knew this, and this concept made its way into their work. In Federalist No. 1, Alexander Hamilton writes, "Of those men who have overturned the liberty of republics, the greatest number have begun their career by paying an obsequious court to the people, commencing demagogues and ending tyrants." And in the last Federalist Paper, No. 85, Hamilton urged the adoption of the Constitution's checks and balances to protect against the "military despotism of a victorious demagogue."

Article I of the Constitution not only allows Congress to impeach the president by a majority vote in the House and convict him by a two-thirds vote in the Senate. It also gives the Senate the opportunity to deliver an additional, more profound remedy, with only a majority vote: "disqualification to hold and enjoy any Office of honor, Trust or Profit under the United States." (On the question of whether Trump can be disqualified after he's a private citizen, the constitutional authority Michael Gerhardt has persuasively argued that a president who "leaves office and retains the potential to return someday should still be subject as well to the unique processes set forth in the Constitution to sanction his abuse of his office." Moreover, as Harvard Law School's Laurence Tribe has recently written, "The clear weight of history, original understanding and congressional practice bolsters the case for concluding that the end of Donald Trump's presidency would not end his Senate trial.")

By giving Americans the drastic option of not only removing an impeached president but permanently excising them from formal politics altogether, the framers were following the ancient model and providing a structural solution to the problem of the demagogue-cum-tyrant.

Trump is the exemplar of the ancient menace, insatiable for power. Too little attention has been paid to the connection between the January 6 putsch and Trump's deployment of federal forces (including DHS personnel and a U.S. Army helicopter) to clear out peaceful protesters in Lafayette Square last summer.

Or his deployment of federal forces in Portland, Oregon, wearing combat fatigues and lacking identification, last summer against Black Lives Matter protesters, in violation of the Posse Comitatus Act preventing the deployment of military forces on domestic soil.

Optimists might think the conviction will be enough, the additional measure of disqualification a bridge too far. But neither Trump nor the mob that supports him has any intention of disappearing from public life. He told us himself, tweeting two days after the putsch: "The 75,000,000 great American Patriots who voted for me, AMERICA FIRST, and MAKE AMERICA GREAT AGAIN, will have a GIANT VOICE long into the future. They will not be disrespected or treated unfairly in any way, shape or form!!!"

And, as the Cook Political Report's Dave Wasserman noted, "If you don't think Donald Trump could reemerge as a formidable candidate for the presidency in four years, you haven't been watching the last four+ years." Moreover, Trump is still quite popular: 74 million Americans voted for him; a recent *HuffPost*/YouGov poll found that 46 percent of Republicans said the insurrectionists "went too far, but they have a point."

Disqualification would recognize Trump not as someone to put in the country's rearview mirror, but as a tumor that must be removed from the body politic. The country is, at this moment, under attack from the very enemy our founders feared most. So we must inoculate democracy with the strongest medicine they gave us. History shows no other way of breaking the cycle that has haunted democracy since its inception.

This essay originally appeared in The Atlantic *on January 16, 2021.*

WHAT THE FOUNDERS WOULD HAVE DONE WITH TRUMP

Frank O. Bowman, III

D onald Trump has now been impeached by the House of Representatives for the second time but will not stand trial before the Senate until after he has left office. Senate backers of the president seem to be coalescing around the argument that at that point their body will no longer have jurisdiction over the by-then ex-president.

The majority of impeachment scholars maintain that the impending trial is perfectly proper. An insistent minority urge the opposite. The arguments so far focus primarily on the text of the Constitution and on three prior impeachments: Senator William Blount who, in 1797-98, was impeached while in office and tried afterward; Secretary of War William Belknap, who in 1876 was both impeached and tried after leaving office; and Judge West Humphreys, who in 1862 was impeached, tried, convicted, and disqualified a year after he abandoned his office to join the Confederacy. Although these impeachments provide persuasive precedent for post-term Senate impeachment jurisdiction, obsessing over them can mislead us because none involved a president. Even though Article II, §4, renders all "civil officers" (a phrase we now read to include judges and executive branch appointees) impeachable, the president was the nearly exclusive focus of all the impeachment debates at the Constitutional Convention.

The delegates supported the ouster of a president for personal corruption, egregious incompetence, and betrayal of the nation to foreign powers. But a singular concern of the framers, not merely when debating impeachment but throughout the process of designing the constitutional system, was the danger of a demagogue rising to the highest office and overthrowing republican government.

When composing our Constitution, the framers drew on their education and studied every historical model they could find. When crafting the impeachment clauses of the Constitution, they focused particularly on the constitutional history of Great Britain and the history of the limited number of prior republics, especially those of ancient Greece and Rome.

The unwritten British constitution was the framers' patrimony. In the wrenching process of resisting and then freeing themselves from British rule, they had studied and debated its every nuance. Likewise, the ancient history of Rome and Greece was the core of the "classical education" almost all the framers possessed to one degree or another, and the educated members of the founding generation drew on their knowledge of it for inspiration and example. Their public and private papers are full of classical allusions. They commonly wrote under pseudonyms of Roman political personalities—Cato, Caesar, Brutus, Agrippa, Cincinnatus, and most famously, Publius, the pen name used by Alexander Hamilton, James Madison, and John Jay as authors of *The Federalist Papers*.

The impeachment mechanism written into the American Constitution owes its structure to a set of very specific lessons the framers drew from British and classical history.

Impeachment was well known to the framers as an invention of the British Parliament, crafted as a legislative tool for resisting royal oppression. Impeachment could not remove the monarch, but it could hobble a ruler's aspirations by removing the ministers who were active agents of royal absolutism. For Parliament, the men most to be feared, who thus became the targets of the great political impeachments, were the hereditary aristocrats and landed gentry who were favorites of the Crown. But such figures could not be entirely defanged merely by removing them from office—even out of office, they retained title, land, wealth, and royal favor and might rise again to threaten constitutional order and, in the violent politics of the times, the very lives of the parliamentarians.

Therefore, the consequences of conviction following a British impeachment included the full range of penalties we would consider criminal – imprisonment, forfeiture of property and title, even death. These stern remedies were not merely retribution for wrongdoing, or even deterrent warnings to future officeholders, but prophylactic measures to ensure that the convicted officer could never again threaten constitutional governance.

The American framers rejected monarchy, and they chose not to create an American aristocracy. Thus, the dangers against which the American rules of impeachment were directed were different. The Framers did not have to worry that an impeached and expelled officer would retain a hereditary title or landed fiefdom from which he could plot a violent resurgence. Nor did they have to worry that such a person would climb back into power by the grace of a hereditary monarch.

Moreover, they did not want the national legislature to act as a court, imposing personal punishments on either private citizens or erring officeholders. But they were every bit as conscious as the British that merely removing an officeholder from power would not necessarily neuter the threat such a person could pose to the Republic. The particular threat that haunted the founding generation was the demagogue.

The founders cautioned against demagogues constantly. The word appears 187 times in the National Archives' database of the founders' writings. Eighteenth-century American writers often used "demagogue" simply as an epithet to suggest that a political opponent was a person of little civic virtue who used the baser arts of flattery and inflammatory rhetoric to secure popular favor. In 1778, in the midst of the Revolution, George Washington wrote to Edward Rutledge complaining that, "that Spirit of Cabal, & destructive Ambition, which has elevated the Factious Demagogue, in every Republic of Antiquity, is making great Head in the Centre of these States."

But the idea at the bottom of the insult was the framers' conclusion, based on the study of history ancient and modern, that republics were peculiarly vulnerable to demagogues – men who craved power for its own sake, and who gained and kept it by dishonest appeals to popular passions.

The framers had ancient historical examples constantly in mind, particularly Cataline, who sought to overturn the Roman Republic by ingratiating himself with the Roman mob and raising an army to make him a dictator. His name was a synonym for anti-republican villainy in the minds of the Revolutionary generation, just as the famous Romans who thwarted him, Cicero and Cato, were the universally admired symbols of steadfast republican virtue.

Alexander Hamilton summed up the founders' view in Federalist No. 1:

"History will teach us, that ... of those men who have overturned the liberties of republics the greatest number have begun their career [sic], by paying an obsequious court to the people, commencing Demagogues and ending Tyrants."

The worry about demagogues influenced every aspect of the constitutional debate. For example, in proposing large, populous districts for members of the House of Representatives, Madison argued they would be less likely to elect demagogues.

The framers' fear of a demagogue was doubly acute because the new American chief executive would be chosen, not by hereditary succession, but the people. The much-maligned electoral college was devised, not only as a means of giving states a special mediating role in picking the president, but also with the idea that the state legislatures tasked with devising processes for picking electors, and the electors themselves, would be sensible statesmen immune to the popular intrigues of a demagogue.

However, the framers expressly rejected the idea that periodic elections alone, even elections by the imagined body of discerning electors, would be sufficient proof against a president either corrupt or with aspirations to tyranny. Accordingly, they adopted impeachment, but with two major innovations from British practice.

The first was making the president, America's head of state and chief executive, subject to impeachment at all. If a demagogue rose to the presidency, he could, upon displaying dangerous behavior redolent of autocratic ambitions, be removed. But Article I, Section 3, does not limit the consequences of conviction to removal. It goes on to permit "disqualification to hold and enjoy any Office of honor, Trust or Profit under the United States."

This provision serves a critical function. Unlike British impeachments of old, impeachment under the federal constitution is not punitive. It is purely political. It seeks to protect the constitutional order in part by removing bad actors from federal service now, *but also*, where appropriate, *by preventing them from rising to power again.* Because the United States has neither a hereditary monarch nor a hereditary landed aristocracy, the officer removed need not be imprisoned or killed to prevent a return to national power. Permanent disqualification suffices. If personal punishments are deserved, those are reserved to the ordinary criminal courts.

How is all this relevant to the apparently technical question of whether a president may be tried after he leaves office?

The key to the founders' fear of the demagogue was not merely that he might secure high office, but that the means by which he would attain it – appeal to the mob – would allow him to corrupt or overthrow the Republic in order to transform himself into a dictator. The source of the demagogue's power does not expire if he is expelled from office; so long as he retains the loyalty of the mob, he may return to power.

As concerned as the framers were about the dangers of the demagogue, they imagined that they were protecting their new Republic in a variety of ways – including a presidential electoral system managed by state political elites and large House districts – that would defeat the wiles of such a person in an age when communication was limited to voice, letters, and newspapers of limited local circulation. Imagine their terror if told of today's technology that allows the demagogue to appeal directly to millions through Facebook, Twitter, Instagram, and YouTube.

Donald Trump is the living embodiment of the framers' fears, amplified many-fold by the reach of modern media technology. If there were any doubt that his departure from the White House will not alone end his threat to the national government, consider that, even now, after the failure of the January 6 assault on the Capitol and the chastisement of a second impeachment,

Washington, D.C., has become a vast armed camp fortified, not against foreign invaders, but against Trump supporters *still* seeking to overturn the results of a free and fair election.

Trump was the man against whom the founding generation armed the Constitution with the disqualification clause. They would surely think anyone quite mad for suggesting that a president who actively sought the overthrow of democracy could not be disqualified from trying again because the failed plot reached its crescendo too close to the expiration of his term.

The Senate trial of Donald Trump for inciting insurrection is entirely consistent with the founders' original intent.

This essay originally appeared in Washington Monthly *on January 18, 2021.*

WOULD THE FOUNDERS CONVICT TRUMP AND BAR HIM FROM OFFICE?

Eli Merritt

If the 55 delegates to the Constitutional Convention in 1787 were sitting today as jurors in the Senate impeachment trial of former President Donald Trump, one thing seems certain based on the historical record. Acting with vigor and dispatch, they would cast two near unanimous votes: first, to convict the president of an impeachable offense, and second, to disqualify him from holding future federal office.

They would vote in this way, unmoved by partisan passions or the defense's claim that the Senate lacks jurisdiction, because they believed as a matter of civic principle that ethical leadership is the glue that holds a constitutional republic together. It was a principle they lived by and one they infused into every aspect of the Constitution they debated that summer in Philadelphia nearly 234 years ago.

As James Madison put it in Federalist No. 57, "The aim of every political constitution is, or ought to be, first to obtain for rulers men who possess most wisdom to discern, and most virtue to pursue, the common good of the society."

In their speeches to the Constitutional Convention, delegates reiterated this point about a constitutional republic's dependence on virtuous leadership almost every day of debates.

Benjamin Franklin highlighted the need to invest the government with "wise and good men." James Wilson wanted "men of intelligence & uprightness." Gouverneur Morris sought "the best, the most able, the most virtuous citizens." And Madison spoke of "impartial umpires & Guardians of justice and general Good."

They also left behind unequivocal statements describing the type of public personalities the constitutional republic must exclude from office. Through carefully designed systems and the power of impeachment, conviction and disqualification, those to be kept out of office included "corrupt & unworthy men," "designing men" and "demagogues," according to Elbridge Gerry.

Alexander Hamilton fought hard to endow the new government with checks and balances to preclude "men of little character," those who "love power" and "demagogues." George Mason devoted himself to devising "the most effectual means of checking and counteracting the aspiring views of dangerous and ambitious men."

Franklin urged the other delegates to add protections in the Constitution to prevent "the bold and the violent, the men of strong passions and indefatigable activity in their selfish pursuits" from ascending to the presidential chair.

Referring to the presidency, Madison warned about the unique risk of "incapacity, negligence or perfidy of the chief Magistrate." He went on to argue, "In the case of the Executive Magistracy, which was to be administered by a single man, loss of capacity or corruption was more within the compass of probable events, and either of them might be fatal to the Republic."

Delegates were concerned with "the public good," "the Natl. peace & harmony," "the internal tranquillity of the States" and "the safety, liberty and happiness of the Community." They intended for the president, as the commander in chief, to pacify civil hatred, resentment and insurrection, not to incite them to hold onto power.

They wrote the language of the impeachment powers with a demagogue like Mr. Trump in mind. As incisive political scientists steeped in history, they understood that demagogues are the singular poison that infects and kills republics and democracies.

As Hamilton warned in Federalist No. 1, these free forms of governments typically die at the hands of ambitious, unscrupulous orators who rise to power on "angry and malignant passions," "avarice, personal animosity, party opposition" and "the bitterness of their invectives." These dangerous politicians, Hamilton said, "have begun their career by paying an obsequious court to the people; commencing demagogues, and ending tyrants."

To safeguard the American people from such politicians, the delegates empowered the House to impeach a president and the Senate both to remove him and to bar him from future office.

Mason was a strong advocate of the Constitution's impeachment powers. On the seventh day of debates, he declared that "some mode of displacing an unfit magistrate" must be incorporated into the national charter for two crucial reasons. One was the "fallibility" of electors, or voters—that is, they might elect a demagogue—and the other, "the corruptibility of the man chosen." In another speech, Mason said of the indispensable instrument of impeachment, "No point is of more importance," and he asked, "Shall any man be above justice?"

What has happened to us today, to our ethics, to our standards of presidential decorum and leadership, to our fidelity to the Constitution and belief in justice, to our political courage and historical understanding of the dangers of demagogues to democracies, for there to be even a remote chance that the Senate, after the Jan. 6 attack on the Capitol, will acquit Mr. Trump, allowing him to run again in 2024?

The revolutionaries who took up arms against King George III were willing to break their bonds with the British Empire and die for the liberties and rights they would write into the Constitution. Today's Republican senators must at least be willing to break with their party and disappoint some of their constituents—and, yes, perhaps lose their jobs in coming elections—to serve the larger interest of protecting the nation.

Those senators who vote to convict and disqualify Mr. Trump will be remembered, in the words of Madison, as "impartial umpires & Guardians of justice and general Good." History will thank them for their integrity, wisdom and honor. They will be lauded, like those who helped create the nation, for the sacrifices they made.

This essay originally appeared in The New York Times *on February 9, 2021.*

TRUMP'S PLACE IN HISTORY? HE IS THE SUPREME AMERICAN DEMAGOGUE

Eli Merritt

D onald Trump's tear across the democratic and constitutional landscape of America is not over. The latest
collateral damage of his lies and attacks is the ouster
of Representative Liz Cheney from her leadership position
as House Republican conference chair. The Republican caucus threw her out because she dares to speak the truth about
Trump's lie that the 2020 presidential election was stolen.

Trump is not going away. The Republican leaders who have
disregarded the truth to enable him should know what future
historians are going to say about the former president—and
them, by association. He will be showcased for decades to come
as the greatest symbol of American demagoguery of all times.
Compared with Trump, demagogues like Huey Long and
Joseph McCarthy will become footnotes.

There is little unique about Trump's methods—which mirror those used by other demagogues—but he has been able
to deploy them all in the most powerful office in the world.
A personality cult, anti-democratic consolidation of power,
populist lies, ceaseless attack on critics, and support for white
supremacy are part of the formula Trump employed to gain
the presidency and secure near-total control of the Republican
Party.

The 20th century offers some relevant historical examples.
Consider the notorious Mississippi demagogue Theodore G.
Bilbo, a Democratic governor who rose to national prominence

in the 1930s on a platform of white supremacy. In striking parallel to Trump's program to build a wall to keep out immigrants he assailed as "drug dealers, criminals, rapists" and "animals," Bilbo was elected to the U.S. Senate twice in part by campaigning against Black equality and interracial marriage.

In 1940, Bilbo's highly publicized program for returning 12 million Black Americans to Africa helped him clinch the Senate for the second time among voters in Jim Crow Mississippi. Bilbo lived by the mantra, "Anything done is all right unless you get caught."

One of the most extraordinary stories in the annals of American demagoguery is that of the Texas husband-and-wife gubernatorial team James E. and Miriam Ferguson. During his second term as governor in 1917, the male Ferguson was impeached, convicted and disqualified from holding future office in the state for misappropriation of public funds and contempt of the Texas Senate.

But this did not stop Ferguson, who had a genius not only for oratory but also for hedging the law. Casting himself as a martyr to corrupt city politics, excoriating the press, Ferguson campaigned hard on behalf of his wife for governor, and she won twice. "The people of Texas," he said on the stump, "will have two governors for the price of one!"

So beloved was Ferguson by his followers that Will Rogers, a humorist of the day, observed, "Jim Ferguson has 150,000 voters in Texas that would be with him if he blew up the Capitol building in Washington."

So too are there abundant similarities in the personalities and political strategies of Trump, Huey Long and Joseph McCarthy. Long, adroit at bullying his way out of impeachment, was an energetic annihilator of democratic and constitutional norms, claiming at one point, "I'm the Constitution around here."

Among the favorite targets of Long, who served as Democratic governor of Louisiana before winning election to the U.S. Senate, was "the lyin' press." He consolidated power over the Democratic Party in his state through verbal assaults, the destruction of careers, the use of military force and patronage reserved only to party members who demonstrate strict, fawning loyalty.

McCarthy, Republican senator from Wisconsin, rose to media prominence by telling preposterous lies about communist infiltration of the State Department and the army. In his 10 years in the Senate, he left countless ruined careers, a severely divided Republican Party and diminished faith among Americans in political leaders and the ethics of government.

Trump's fate in history is to become the superstar in this cast of dishonored political figures. He will be remembered as the first full-blown demagogue in the White House, one who incited seditious violence on the U.S. Capitol—and for little else. Over time, Democrats and Republicans will unite in this historical understanding of Trump, just as they have long since reached consensus about Democrat Huey Long and Republican Joseph McCarthy. The judgment of Trump will not be a partisan matter.

If Republican leaders care about how history will judge them, they need to join Cheney in the determined fight to put truth and the health of our democracy above party and power. In the long arc of history, truth always wins over demagoguery.

This essay originally appeared in The Los Angeles Times *on May 12, 2021.*

MY FELLOW REPUBLICANS, STOP FEARING THIS DANGEROUS AND DIMINISHED MAN

Barbara Comstock

W hen Donald Trump, the patron saint of sore losers, appeared at a Republican event on Saturday night and compared the 2020 election to a "third-world-country election like we've never seen before," it wasn't just another false rant from the former president. His words also described his attempted subversion of democracy in the run-up to the Jan. 6 riot at the Capitol.

Consider Mr. Trump's remarks at his rally just before the attack: "If Mike Pence does the right thing, we win the election," he said. "All Vice President Pence has to do is send it back to the states to recertify and we become president."

Or consider Mr. Trump's harassment of Georgia's Republican secretary of state, Brad Raffensperger, with the request to "find" him votes, or his relentless harassment of other election officials and governors.

Many Republicans want to move on from the Jan. 6 attack. But how is that possible when the former president won't move on from the Nov. 3 election and continues to push the same incendiary lies that resulted in 61 failed lawsuits before Jan. 6, led to an insurrection and could lead to yet more violence?

If you doubt that a threat of violence exists, look at the recent poll from the Public Religion Research Institute and the Interfaith Youth Core, which shows that a dangerous QAnon conspiracy theory is believed by 15 percent of our fellow Americans—including almost one in four Republicans, 14 percent of independents and even 8 percent of Democrats.

Republicans, instead of opposing a commission to investigate the events of Jan. 6, need to be at the forefront of seeking answers on the insurrection and diminishing the power of QAnon and the other conspiracy theories that Mr. Trump has fueled. While he is still popular within the party, Mr. Trump is a diminished political figure: 66 percent of Americans now hope he won't run again in 2024, including 30 percent of Republicans. He is not the future, and Republicans need to stop fearing him. He will continue to damage the party if we don't face the Jan. 6 facts head-on.

Nothing less than a full investigation is essential. As a House Republican chief counsel during the Clinton administration, I see a clear set of unanswered questions about Jan. 6, as well as evidence that needs to be gathered and that our country needs to understand. An investigation should cover the events related and leading up to Jan. 6, as well as all the parties involved. Who planned and funded the Trump rally that day, and who picked the speakers and got attendees there? How did supporters of QAnon, Oath Keepers and the Proud Boys get there? What happened as the White House planned for Jan. 6?

Whether it is a congressionally formed commission or a congressional committee, the subpoenas and testimony would produce records that tell the story. Imagine all the thousands of texts, emails, phone calls and other records from the weeks leading to and on Jan. 6 that are not yet part of the public record. This material will come out eventually—in hearings, in books or in the media—but Republicans should be part of the process, to help provide accountability and prevent future attacks.

While a commission would be best, a congressional select committee with a five-Democrat, five-Republican split and the same rules as a commission would have, could also work. In the meantime, any standing committee with subpoena power could begin the information-gathering process immediately.

Many Republican leaders seem to think any all-encompassing investigation will be bad for the party. I disagree. Some prominent Republicans want to uncover the truth, as do police officers who heroically protected members of Congress and their staff on Jan. 6. Officer Brian Sicknick, who died after engaging with the Trump-inspired mob, supported Mr. Trump. Officer Michael Fanone, who was shocked multiple times with a stun gun and beaten and suffered a heart attack and traumatic brain injury, told me he is a Republican. Officer Harry Dunn said: "We were victims of an assault, of an attack, and we deserve justice and we deserve to know everybody who was involved, and we want them held accountable." Many of our officers feel they are being left on the field, and they wonder, what happened to "Back the Blue."

Mr. Trump's lies are red meat to those in the conspiracy world who have already demonstrated what they are prepared to do. The danger also extends to states, as Mr. Trump tells people that election outcomes in Georgia and Arizona will be overturned, and he could be reinstated as president in August. How will QAnon followers or Oath Keepers respond when that does not happen?

Many Republicans rationalize ignoring his rhetoric: His speech on Saturday wasn't even aired live on Fox or CNN, and he may end up being indicted in New York and occupied with legal and financial problems. So, this thinking goes, what's the harm in humoring the guy a little longer?

The harm is that the lies have metastasized and could threaten public safety again. The U.S. Capitol Police report that threats against members of Congress have increased 107 percent this year. Representative Adam Kinzinger, a Republican, has noted, "There's no reason to believe that anybody organically is going to come to the truth." Representative Liz Cheney, another Republican, said, "It's an ongoing threat, so silence is not an option."

Humoring the guy also emboldens Mr. Trump's pardoned allies like Steve Bannon and his former national security adviser Michael Flynn. Republicans are now flocking to Mr. Bannon's podcast to audition for Mr. Trump's support, and Mr. Bannon says "a litmus test" will be whether they are willing to challenge the outcome of the 2020 election. Later this month, Mr. Flynn will appear at an Oklahoma campaign rally with Jackson Lahmeyer, a political novice who is challenging Senator James Lankford, the Republican incumbent. Mr. Lahmeyer claims the 2020 election was stolen and touts Mr. Flynn's endorsement, saying we have to be willing to "Fight Like a Flynn."

Republicans would be better advised to fight like Senator Margaret Chase Smith. During the Joseph McCarthy era in 1950, she advised fellow Republicans that the Democrats had already provided Republicans with sufficient campaign issues, and they need not resort to McCarthy's demagogy.

The same is true today. Republicans need to have more faith in their policies and stop being afraid of a dangerous and diminished man who has divided the country and now divides our party. Reconsider the commission, let the investigation go ahead, and run and win in 2022 on the truth.

This essay originally appeared in The New York Times *on June 9, 2021.*

A DAY OF IGNOMINY IN THE U.S. SENATE, ONE YEAR LATER: REMEMBERING TRUMP'S IMPEACHMENT ACQUITTAL

Eli Merritt

L
ast month, Americans observed the first anniversary of the Jan. 6 assault on the U.S. Capitol, a tragic day in our history. However, by the crucial measure of the strength of civic virtue among our elected officials, another day, Feb. 13, should be highlighted as one of even greater consequence for the security and stability of our democracy.

On Saturday, Feb. 13, 2021, 43 Republican senators voted to acquit President Donald Trump of the charge of incitement of the insurrection, thereby thwarting a conviction by the required two-thirds majority. By not convicting and then disqualifying Trump from holding future federal office, those 43 senators single-handedly enabled one of the most destructive politicians in U.S. history to campaign again for president and to return to the White House for a second term.

Knowingly, on Feb. 13, these Republican senators placed partisan attachment to an authoritarian demagogue over the Constitution, the truth and the safety of the American people. In that crucial hour, they failed to uphold their sworn duty to "support and defend the Constitution of the United States against all enemies, foreign and domestic."

The senators committed this grave error not on grounds of any reasonable interpretation of law or oath, but because they could not muster sufficient civic virtue within themselves to elevate the best interests of the nation over self-interest and party.

No American should think for a moment that civic virtue is an obsolete moral principle best left to the idealism of the classroom. No, it is the lifeblood of democracy, no matter the historic point in time. When this vital substance dries up in the leadership of a republican form of government, there is little hope for the preservation of freedom, justice, equality, rule of law and peace among the people.

The reason for the surpassing importance of civic virtue in our elected officials is that no other deep element of government or human nature can possibly withstand the tempestuous aggressions of an authoritarian demagogue, like Trump, upon our democratic institutions and values.

The principle of civic virtue, promoted as a *sine qua non* of democratic self-government since ancient Athens, has broad meaning and applications, including injunctions to citizens to honesty, respect, service, patriotism, benevolence, forbearance, self-sacrifice and courage.

More to the point, though, in the case of U.S. senators casting a historic vote to hold an authoritarian demagogue from their own party accountable for overt efforts to overturn a free and fair election—or to let him off scot-free—the field of responsibility narrows chiefly to the twin duties of self-sacrifice and courage.

We do not have to look far to find instances of the anguished exercise of these two duties in the Senate. Seven Republican senators on that day understood the depth of the authoritarian crisis confronting the nation and, searching their consciences, chose to lay down their political lives and reputations for the Constitution and the preservation of our democracy.

Those senators were Richard Burr of North Carolina, Bill Cassidy of Louisiana, Susan Collins of Maine, Lisa Murkowski of Alaska, Mitt Romney of Utah, Ben Sasse of Nebraska and Pat Toomey of Pennsylvania.

"That attack was not a spontaneous outbreak of violence," Collins explained shortly after her vote on Feb. 13, speaking truth to Trump's lies. "Rather, it was the culmination of a steady stream of provocations by President Trump that were aimed at overturning the results of the presidential election.

"Rather than defend the constitutional transfer of power," she continued, "he incited an insurrection with the purpose of preventing that transfer of power from occurring." She concluded, "My vote in this trial stems from my own oath and duty to defend the Constitution of the United States."

Sasse, in a statement issued the same day, underscored the fact that lies about an election outcome promulgated by a president conspicuously risk political violence and, as such, are sufficient grounds for conviction.

Regarding Trump's two lies about a stolen election and Vice President Mike Pence's authority to overturn the election, Sasse explained, "Those lies had consequences, endangering the life of the vice president and bringing us dangerously close to a bloody constitutional crisis. Each of these actions are violations of a president's oath of office."

Five days later, Romney entered a statement into the Congressional Record asserting that it is the Senate's responsibility "to hold accountable those who abuse their office or threaten our Republic." He voted for conviction, he said, because "I consider an attempt to corrupt an election to keep oneself in power one of the most reprehensible acts that can be taken by a sitting president."

Feb. 13, 2021, marks a day to remember not because seven Republican senators roused the courage to put the Constitution and public safety before party and political self-preservation, but because 43 did not. Instead of standing up for our democracy and, vitally, for domestic peace, they recklessly empowered Trump to rise again as a candidate for the presidency.

As a nation, with time, we should forgive the senators, but we must not forget. We must not forget that they held in their hands a constitutional power to permanently exclude an authoritarian demagogue from federal electoral politics. We do not yet know the full consequences of the senators' votes that day, but we must hold them accountable for their dereliction of duty.

This essay originally appeared in The New York Daily News *on February 13, 2022.*

DEMOCRACY'S SURVIVAL DEPENDS ON FIGHTING DEMAGOGUES. HERE'S WHY

Eli Merritt

The House select committee's investigation of the Jan. 6 insurrection has hammered home a fundamental truth about democracy. This cherished form of government, rooted in the will of the people, can be upended by demagogues when political party gatekeepers do not block their ascent to power.

When gatekeepers fail in this critical duty, democracies deteriorate in a process well-known to political philosophers throughout history, including Alexander Hamilton. As he wrote in Federalist No. 1, such individuals achieve elected power by manipulating and dividing the people, "commencing demagogues, and ending tyrants."

In other words, the first step in democratic breakdown is the election of a demagogue to power. Such a person, as Eric A. Posner explains in *The Demagogue's Playbook*, is one "who obtains the support of the people through dishonesty, emotional manipulation, and the exploitation of social divisions; who targets the political elites, blaming them for everything that has gone wrong; and who tries to destroy institutions—legal, political, religious, social—and other sources of power that stand in their way."

Once in office, the demagogue devolves into an authoritarian who subverts the government, corrupting and dismantling the democracy itself to retain power.

Donald Trump started out as a demagogue, and, as the recent House hearings show, he slid deep into authoritarianism, orchestrating an aggressive multifaceted campaign to overturn a free and fair election. What the United States and the world have witnessed over the past seven years since Trump announced his run for president is precisely the process of democratic deterioration that takes place when gatekeepers neglect to fulfill their duty to keep demagogues out of the executive pipeline.

Demagogues are as ancient as democracy itself, and, historically, watchful gatekeepers prevent them from seizing the bully pulpit and winning the public trust. Gatekeepers need to have eagle eyes for spotting this corrupting subset of political actors. Then they must work to sideline them by all means permissible, public and private.

Since the early years of the American republic, elected and appointed officials, judges, journalists and community leaders have assumed this gatekeeping role, but none of these compare in importance to the central role of political parties. In our system of government, each party has the crucial duty of defending the Constitution against demagogues. Before anything else, that means ensuring that a party's presidential nominee demonstrates an unwavering commitment to free and fair elections and the peaceful transfer of power.

As Steven Levitsky and Daniel Ziblatt, authors of *How Democracies Die*, assert, "an essential test for democracies is not whether such figures emerge but whether political leaders, and especially political parties, work to prevent them from gaining power in the first place—by keeping them off mainstream party tickets, refusing to endorse or align with them and, when necessary, making common cause with rivals in support of democratic candidates."

Some might protest that this gatekeeping by political parties is antidemocratic. But no system of government is perfect. That democracy can degenerate into tyranny through freely elected demagogues is an abiding paradox. It is democracy's inconvenient truth—its greatest burden and most vexing dilemma.

Today, the Republican Party is duty bound to defend our democracy and Constitution against further assault by Trump. If the party of Lincoln does not stand up for candidates committed to free and fair elections and the peaceful transfer of power, it stands for nothing at all. Its failure to reject Trump resulted in institutional breakdown—and violence. And that is what will continue to happen if the party does not act decisively.

Recovery from the political trauma of the insurrection must begin with holding Trump accountable for his role in trying to overturn the 2020 election. But to safeguard our democracy from future presidential candidates who seek to take the same path, the leaders of both parties must embrace their duty to thwart such corrupt politicians at every turn.

Grasping this truth—that each party is responsible for counteracting its own demagogues—is a crucial starting point for rescuing American democracy from further decline.

This essay originally appeared in The Los Angeles Times *on August 9, 2022.*

About the Editor

Eli Merritt is a psychiatrist and political historian at Vanderbilt University who has written political commentary and historical analysis for *The American Journal of Legal History*, *The New York Times*, *Los Angeles Times*, *Seattle Times*, *Chicago Tribune*, and *Philadelphia Inquirer*, among other publications. He writes a Substack newsletter called *American Commonwealth* that explores the origins of the United States' political discontents and solutions to them.

His areas of academic expertise are ethical leadership in democracy, the intersection of demagogues and democracy, and the politics of the founding era of the United States. Trained in history and ethics at Yale and psychiatry at Stanford, he has also written about medical and psychiatric ethics and served on medical ethics committees at Stanford and Vanderbilt.

He is the editor of *How to Save Democracy: Advice and Inspiration from 96 World Leaders*, scheduled for publication in 2023. His book *Disunion Among Ourselves: The Perilous Politics of the American Revolution* is also scheduled for publication in 2023.

Learn more about these books and his other writings online at elimerritt.com and elimerritt.substack.com.